M000312558

# DISRUPTIVE SUCCESSOR

# DISRUPTIVE SUCCESSOR

## A GUIDE FOR DRIVING GROWTH IN YOUR FAMILY BUSINESS

JONATHAN GOLDHILL

HOUNDSTOOTH
PRESS



DISRUPTIVE SUCCESSOR
*A Guide for Driving Growth in Your Family Business*

ISBN 978-1-5445-1703-2 *Hardcover*
978-1-5445-1570-0 *Paperback*
978-1-5445-1569-4 *Ebook*

# CONTENTS

# INTRODUCTION

At twenty-six years old, Justin White was an estimator, project manager, and tractor operator at K&D Landscaping, his parents' commercial landscape construction and maintenance company. Justin and his younger brother, Shane, kind of grew up in the business. As youngsters, they would ride along to jobs with their dad, sitting in the back of the truck. When he was eighteen, Justin started working more steadily at K&D, learning the business, and moving slowly toward leading it alongside the founders—his parents. At that time, his mother and father had built up the small mom-and-pop operation for over twenty years, up to ten employees. By 2008, just before the financial crisis, they peaked at close to $2M in revenues. Then business shrunk back to closer to $1M per year, with inconsistent profitability.

That's when I met Justin. He was eager to become the CEO of the business and had a vague vision to grow the business while improving its stability, people (by hiring better employees and upgrading current employees' skills and capacity), and profitability. His parents were proud of the company they'd built, satisfied with the success they had attained, and not yet ready to turn the reins over to him. So they weren't all that sold on Justin's plans. They didn't feel any need to make significant changes. With one big exception: as Justin was about to learn when I first met him, his parents were going to divorce.

With that, the company was changing—starting with the company buying out his mother's stock, a big deal for any small company, with extra layers of complication when it's a family company—and Justin was in the thick of it. And, honestly, he was in uncharted territory. Really honestly, so were all the family members running K&D. They were adept at running a small landscape business, but that did not mean they were prepared for what was to come.

## THE DISRUPTIVE SUCCESSOR

It's not easy to navigate the process of becoming a next-generation leader by taking over the management of a business from your parents. And it's not much easier to hand over the reins to your children. Any kind of change is difficult. Humans just don't love it. It feels risky. So much the more so when your goal is to take the company away from the status quo by aiming for more growth or a different way of doing things: when you are a disruptive successor.

The challenges can be psychological, dealing with family dynamics, but they are also almost always based on fundamental business practices. And that's good news. All the pieces about optimizing the way the business runs are coachable! There are tools; there are methods and strategies. You can learn to use them! No matter where you are now, with the right support, you can not only weather any transition but also take the company—your company—to new heights.

Following concrete steps to unlock the full potential of your business comes with a valuable bonus: you can transcend the kind of rivalry that plagues many family businesses. I know all this is possible because I've seen it done time and time again. It's why I wrote this book: I want everyone to be able to do the same for their family's business.

If you are looking to grow your family business and successfully guide that growth for years to come, this book will give you the strategies, tools, and techniques you need. And if what you're aiming for is to build a better business that is more valuable and more sellable or more ready to pass along to the next generation, then this book is for you, too. And this book is for you if you are determined to grow personally and professionally along with the business so that you can learn more, earn more, work less, and enjoy the climb to success.

## PUT ME IN, COACH

It took a bit of convincing to get his parents on board with hiring a coach (that's me), but Justin was determined to educate himself about the best way to grow their business and find someone to mentor him as a leader. To him, it seemed urgent as K&D approached this intergenerational transfer of power.

We started by pinning down a specific goal: Justin wanted to be running a \$5M-per-year company within five years. Next up was developing Justin's skillset and mindset—this involved reading several books I've found to be the most helpful over the years—so that he would be prepared to reach this goal. Later, we called it his Big Hairy Audacious Goal or BHAG®[1] to reach \$30M by 2030. To define the path—and keep him on it—we built a detailed but straightforward one-page business plan.

Justin decided on several action items and began checking them off his list.

1. Develop and implement efficient systems for sales, marketing estimating, and billing/invoicing, and create a recruitment system to qualify and hire valuable employees. DONE.
2. Hire experienced managers to delegate everyday tasks he and his father were performing. DONE.
3. Develop the maintenance division as a self-sustaining division requiring little oversight and utilizing systems and specific job descriptions for foremen and managers. DONE.
4. Create a better quality of life for his family and himself. DONE.
5. Create an exit plan for each of the founders so they have specific milestones to hit as they near retirement (an eight- to ten-year retirement goal). IN PROGRESS.

## TRANSITION IS THE TRICKY PART

The majority of America's wealth lies with family-owned businesses, and the longevity is impressive! According to the Conway Center for Family Business, the average family-controlled company is in the family's hands for over sixty years, meaning the tenure of leadership in a family enterprise is four to five times longer than in other companies.[2]

In transferring leadership from generation to generation, however, family businesses go from startups to structured, complex organizations. This is the most challenging transition for family businesses; not all will succeed.

So you'll be glad to have a guide with you on this journey,

because although almost 70% of family businesses would like to pass their business on to the next generation, only 30% successfully do so. Less than 1 in 3! Furthermore, only 13% are still viable into the third generation. And only 3% of all family businesses are operating into the fourth generation and beyond.

And yet, according to studies, 62% of family leaders plan to pass the business on to the next generation. And 39% will pass on leadership within the next five years. Also, according to the 2019 PWC US Family Business Survey, 75% of next-generation leaders report having ambitious plans to take the business to the next level when they take over.[3]

These are the disruptive successors!

"Right, I'm the 1 in 3," you might think. "I'm different. I'm full of enthusiasm, great ideas, and experience!" I don't doubt that you are, but it's incredibly likely that the 70% who failed were also excited about the opportunity they had been given and had plenty of great ideas and experience as well.

If you would like to grow your business, make it more profitable, and then successfully transfer it to your children, having a roadmap through the transition process makes it much more likely that you'll be able to pick up where your parents left off and capitalize on their success.

You'll bring enthusiasm and energy that your folks may no longer have. Maybe you want to try new ways of running your business and take more risks. Perhaps you are excited to set your sights higher and invest in a bigger future. You may want to buy land, machinery, inventory, or equipment or expand to other locations. Perhaps you want to work remotely, relocate to another part of the state or country, have more work-life balance, take more time off, and enjoy a better life. Or possibly start another business. And you might want to use your parents' business and financial resources to pay for some of this.

If you genuinely are a **disruptive** successor, you'll have a different vision from that of your forebears. You may already be known for your desire to achieve, your ability to innovate, and your aspirations for substantial growth. You need to bring a kind of "creative destruction" in order to overhaul production processes and increase your family business's competitiveness.

Because the founders view you as young, to them your mindset might seem all about the short term. So you will have to demonstrate that you have a clear long-term vision focusing on ambitious but attainable goals. If there is one trait that defines successful entrepreneurs, it is their obsession with results and the feeling that there is always a new challenge to overcome. Now is your defining moment—one that may take years to demonstrate but can be your legacy.

There are endless books out there on how to scale up a business. But very few of them are written for the next-generational family member of an entrepreneurial founder in a multigenerational business—**the disruptive successor**. That's why I've written this guide for those who are gearing up for intergenerational transitions in family businesses, facing the reality that few succeed, and determined to beat the odds.

Even when transitions are successful, they are tricky to manage. Parents and children have different needs. Sometimes they don't understand their situation in the same way.

The older generation may be focused on leaving a legacy, while their successors are thinking about earning a living, supporting their family, sustaining a certain quality of life, and potentially providing for other family members if/when they can't provide for themselves.

A trusted advisor, whether it's a mentor, peer, family accountant or attorney, exit or succession planner, business coach, or all of the above, can make the difference between success and failure. This book aims to take on those roles. Of course, it can't do everything a live person can to tailor advice to your exact situation, but it does lay out a roadmap that can point any business in the right direction.

## MISSION ACCOMPLISHED AND CONTINUING

After K&D made it through the major transition in 2016, including buying out Justin's mom, and making Justin a newly minted CEO, Justin and his dad were fully convinced of the value of outside business coaching.

Five years later, K&D's growth has exceeded even Justin's original vision. Revenues have grown almost 10x with a healthy and consistent net profit. Even better, he's built a team of talented, committed leaders. Working with his brother, who shares his thirst for excellence, Justin is attracting more and more talent to the business—in an industry that is short on talent. The crowning achievements are all the awards, articles, and accolades they are earning in their community and industry—setting them apart from their competitors.

And Justin's still on that mission to scale to $30M. Now that he's come this far, the goal is looking a lot less big and hairy and a lot more like the next logical step.

## THE FOUNDERS' ROLE IN SUCCESSION

I have written this book for the next-generation leader or aspiring leader who wants to understand how to transition into leadership and run the family business. But it is also for the founding-generation leader (founder) exploring how to successfully transfer the business to the next generation. It may also be of use to "transgenerational entrepreneurs"—those who went out on their own and started a different business maybe in a different industry from their family's business.

To all you next-generation leaders, I'm assuming your parent(s) built a decent business. And now that you and maybe your sibling(s) have joined the company full time, it needs to grow to support all of you and produce much more income. You may see the business's potential and have bigger ambitions still. Either way, being a successor is being a disruptive successor: things are going to be different around here.

If you are a founder whose children work for your company, then you may want to understand what will be required for your next-generation leader to scale your business. You may be considering your exit plan and the next chapter of your life. Do you continue to grow the business? Have you run out of steam? Will your children be able to take your business to new heights of revenue and profitability? Or should you sell it and exit the company? This book will teach you some new tools, many of which you can implement yourself if you still have the energy, motivation, and drive. Or you can mentor your children and gain clarity on if they have what it takes to take over the reins or if they'll be better off if you sell. Either way, this book is for you.

I'm speaking mostly to businesses that generate or will soon generate at least $1M in revenues. Otherwise, the implementation of my recommendations might be overwhelming. And the prime target of this book is those $1M+ businesses with 10 to 250 employees where owners aspire to be making $30M or more in annual revenues.

## I'VE BEEN WHERE YOU ARE

I would have been in your shoes had my family's substantial wholesale manufacturing company, Joseph H. Cohen & Sons (JHC), survived past the third generation. My family ran one of the largest industrial firms in Philadelphia. My great-grandfather, Joseph H. Cohen—a Jewish immigrant from Eastern Europe—was the founder, and his sons—Willie, Izzy, and George—joined the family business full time right out of high school, if not earlier. JHC grew very large during World War II. It leased and eventually purchased the old Ford motor plant in north Philadelphia (later renamed the Botany 500 building). In 1965, after forty-one years of ownership by the Cohen family, Meshulam Riklis's Rapid-American Corp. purchased JHC for over $21M, retained the name, its management staff, and its key employees. My grandfather and his brother were given lifetime employment contracts as CEO and CAO. In 1966, JHC signed a government contract to produce military uniforms and expanded to 3,100 employees in that same building. In 1973, JHC bought out the Botany 500 brand, whose name became well known after the company styled many popular TV show hosts. JHC outlasted many US-based clothing companies during a time when the manufacturing of men's suits was increasingly moving to countries where labor was cheaper and more abundant. Eventually, because of the significant decline in production in Philadelphia in the 1970s and 1980s, the advancing years of my grandfather and his two brothers, and a lack of interest from the next generation of family members, JHC ceased operations and production in 1986.[4]

Had they retained the business and made the shift to overseas manufacturing, I might have ended up in the position of trying to figure out how to continue it through the fourth generation of family members and overcome declining consumer interest in men's suits and dress clothes.

My first business struggles came, not coincidentally, also in the clothing business. The Venice Beach, California, business I founded with a wearable art clothing artist and designer seemed destined to succeed given my family history and my entrepreneurial enthusiasm. But our success was short-lived—eventually we failed because our partnership went awry. Had we been family or shared a vision, we might have succeeded. Instead, as time would reveal, we were just crossing paths in life.

You learn more from your failures than your successes, as they say, and this experience sent me off to graduate school to get my MBA in entrepreneurship and cement those learnings. But my real challenges were yet to come. Degree in hand, I joined a small consulting company, which dissolved around me when the executive director retired one year later and all our contracts dried up. The three people remaining at the company—including me—were left to save the business. We borrowed $10,000 from the local chamber of commerce, and less than ten years later, we had built a nationally recognized firm with over $7M in assets, $4M in annual contracts, and more than thirty workers. Looking back, this was my disruptive successor story, although not in a family business.

> *"If you really look closely, most overnight successes took a long time."*
>
> —STEVE JOBS, ENTREPRENEUR, FOUNDER OF APPLE INC.

Ten years later, looking to move into a more entrepreneurial field, I jumped into a fast-growing digital media event management company as COO. But my timing could not have been worse! Less than one year later, the dot-com bubble burst and took the company out and with it a good chunk of my stock portfolio. So I went back to consulting and slowly, over time, scraped my way back to a successful home-based consulting services business that supported my family. Once I went out on my own as a solopreneur, I never looked back. But it wasn't easy in the early years to market my consulting and coaching business to small and medium-sized corporations. So many of my efforts didn't pan out! I know the pain of trying to grow a business.

As I built up my consulting practice and made the transition to becoming a business coach, I learned what struggles most business owners have in common in terms of their struggles. I had experienced many of them myself, and I was rapidly discovering how widespread they were. Case after case, I was working with founders on:

- Time Management
- Priority Management
- Goal Setting
- Results Tracking

- Work-Life Balance Integration
- Leadership and People Management
- Financial Knowledge
- Marketing and Selling
- Operations, Systems, and Process Management

Once I recognized the framework, it was easier to get owners to see how their business fit into a pattern—and how I could give them the tools they needed to solve their challenges. I didn't need to teach each person a specific way to fix their problems. It was much better to teach owners the basics of people management, priority and time management, marketing strategy, and financial management so they could diagnose and cure whatever came up for them. These were foundational skills. Still, many businesses manage to roll along without them for a long time. And that's fine. I can't argue with success. But are you aiming to take that success to a new level? If so, go back to basics; laying a healthy foundation is the best way to start any building.

With this new approach, I began finding my success right alongside that of my clients. Often, even simple changes to their businesses yielded significant results.

It doesn't matter what your business is or what its practices have looked like up until now. This book can guide you in finding ways to optimize, paving the way not just for a successful transition but also for continuing growth.

If you want to build a fantastic family business, you'll need a whole bevy of critical pieces in place. You'll want a process that makes the founder confident the company will transition into good hands—and the successor confident their hands will be good! That means you'll need a strategic roadmap that guides the whole process and can be communicated down through every level of the company so you can take your family business and scale it even beyond what your family originally envisioned.

You'll need the best tools possible to help you get there—that is, tools that go beyond what you learned by watching and working for the founder. I don't say that lightly, knowing that the founder has probably taught you so much of what you know in business—and in life. A next-generation leader bent on making real change—what I call a *disruptive successor*—needs a bigger toolbox.

Most of this book is about my 7 P's Playbook for managing your business. Those 7 P's, which we'll call the **Family Leader's Playbook** are **Purpose, Plan, Products, People, Priorities, Processes,** and **Performance**. They're what any business needs to grow big enough to dominate its industry. The playbook provides a structure to facilitate growth, and controlled management of growth, and backs it up with all the necessary tools. Each P gets a chapter, or chapters, to lay out what it means to your business and how to improve it, no matter your starting point.

If you implement the P's as suggested, they should add significant value to your business. The tools I share will help you manage your time and priorities better, focus your team on the business plan and quarterly priorities, improve the health of your team, coach your managers, and everything else it takes to grow your business.

At the end of most chapters, you will find specific action items using the tools you just learned. These will allow you to start improving your business right away, though I predict you will return to many of them again and again over time. Some of these business growth tools will be available as downloads from my website, and I periodically add new ones: www.DisruptiveSuccessor.com. Do not ignore these tools or skip the exercises associated with them. They have proven effective over and over again.

Throughout all the chapters, you'll see more stories like Justin's journey taking over his family's landscaping firm. To me, these are powerful teaching moments, these real-life examples of family businesses scaling up, driving value, exit planning, training successors, and continuing the founders' legacy down through the generations. I hope they will help you to see—and then inspire you to aim for—all that is possible.

# CHAPTER 1

# WHAT GOT YOU HERE WON'T GET YOU THERE

## THE 7 P'S PLAYBOOK EVERY FAMILY BUSINESS NEEDS TO SCALE UP

*"If you want to teach people a new way of thinking, don't bother trying to teach them. Instead, give them a tool, the use of which will lead to new ways of thinking."*

—BUCKMINSTER FULLER, AMERICAN ARCHITECT, SYSTEMS THEORIST, FUTURIST

The world has changed a lot since your founder started and grew the business. If the company is operating well with a decent foundation under it, then there is unlimited potential for you to take the reins and create expansive growth. But success is neither quick nor easy.

You and your founder(s) must recognize that the world of business has changed over the years. Digitization and other technological advancements have disrupted how we do business and even transformed entire industries. So what got your founder here won't get you there. Taking your business where you want it to go will require a new set of tools, a more strategic mindset, and some fresh entrepreneurial energy. You bring the raw power, and I'm presenting the rest to you in this book.

We are witnessing the most significant generational transfer of businesses and wealth ever, from baby boomers to Gen X and millennials. According to the US Census Bureau, baby boomers own about two-thirds of businesses with employees in the United States—about 4 million companies[5]—and have already begun to put their companies on the market and will continue to do so into 2030.

Family businesses are a bit unique here. A sizable percentage of owners transfer their business to the next generation of family members. An estimated 40% of these family business owners expect to retire[6]—creating a significant transition of ownership in the process—but almost half of family business owners have no succession plan in place. And only 20 to 30% of all businesses that are put on the market ever sell![7]

Why do so many family businesses have no robust succession plan—that is, a documented and communicated leadership transition strategy—in place? Perhaps it's because the needs of the next generation are not well understood and can appear at odds with the needs of the preceding generation. By using tools and techniques of concrete business planning, like the ones in this book, you can get everyone on the same page.

Businesses preparing for transition now face global and technological factors that weren't issues for the founders' generation. Yet, less than 10% of successors think their family's business has a strategy for operating in our technological age. The skills needed in the next iteration of your business are not the same ones the founding generation used. The Internet of Things has transformed our world. Misunderstanding the need to leap into digital can be deadly to business succession.

Typically, my clients have been small businesses with under 500 employees. Although each client has their own specific needs and wants, usually they are coming to me looking for more growth—specifically, more income, sales, and cash flow—as well as more freedom, fun, and fulfillment.

## THE DISRUPTIVE SUCCESSORS ARE COMING

A global survey of next-generation family businesses conducted in 2016 by Deloitte yielded some interesting findings. The next generation of family business leaders intends to make changes when they take over:

- 80% say their leadership style will be different from the previous generation's
- 56% will change the family company's strategy
- 56% will improve corporate governance structures
- 51% intend to take more risk than their predecessors but in a more controlled way
- 76% say innovation is a top three priority for the next-generation leader
- 55% say their companies innovate at a faster pace than the competition
- 61% of previous-generation family members are well aware of the need for innovation

BUT

- 40% are not so willing to take on the associated risks

So how do you stack up against these statistics?

Are you a next-generation leader taking over a family business? Are you disrupting the equilibrium of the business by requesting that the ownership structure and decision making pass on from one generation to the next?

If this is the case, then perhaps you're a merchant-builder innovator—for example, a team builder, salesperson, deal maker, or technology innovator. Maybe you lead through inspiration and excitement. Perhaps you are a builder type—that is, someone with the drive to build a highly scalable business and grow it fast.

If your parent or grandparent built a business, you are disruptive to want to take it to a new level. Although some parents might appreciate this, many feel threatened by it. The fact is that you have a lot to offer. Whatever you learned from your parents was a great start, but it probably isn't going to get the business to that next level of success. You are going to have to pioneer by bringing unfamiliar ideas, methods, tools, and technologies to the company, which is going to take some disruption. Although beneficial, adopting new behaviors is always going to meet with some resistance. You will need to find new people (employees, advisors, and shareholders) who are excited by change and innovation. And you will probably have to say goodbye to some of the older folks who were more comfortable with the business the way it was.

## THREE TYPES OF INNOVATIONS

There are three types of innovation that you will want to consider. They are product innovation, process innovation, and business model innovation.

### 1. PRODUCT INNOVATION

Product innovation is the creation and introduction of something that is either new or an improved version of something old. Years ago, my friend was searching to buy a business. When he landed upon a new hamburger franchise, I initially thought, why is he buying a hamburger business? Does the world really need another hamburger business? But this business was very different. They offered custom-topped gourmet burgers with over a million possible combinations. It was an example of product innovation, which has been imitated by many other competitors and carried them as a market leader for almost two decades.

The smartwatch category is another in which we have seen many product innovations. In 1946, the comic book detective Dick Tracy had a two-way wristwatch radio. The tech took a long time to catch up to what this fictitious character had, but it's here now. In 2007, Fitbit introduced wearable technology devices to measure fitness, sleep, steps climbed, and more. In 2015, Apple released its first smartwatches, while Samsung, a forerunner in the category, did the same in 2013. These watches were a radical innovation. Many people put aside their analog Rolexes, Timexes, and Seikos in favor of watches that could set alarms, read email, make phone calls, give you driving directions, and track your fitness.

### 2. PROCESS INNOVATION

Process innovation is a type of change that, although more obscure to the casual observer, usually results in reduced costs of production and improvement to the end product. Examples of process innovation include Amazon's personalization, which makes suggestions based on your buying history, and

Henry Ford's invention of the moving assembly line, which reduced assembly time from hours to minutes. Minnesota Manufacturing & Mining, the company now known as 3M and the inventors of Scotch® tape, Scotchgard™, Thinsulate™, and Post-it® Notes, may have failed at mining, but they've succeeded at innovation. Their goal is to have 30% of their revenue come from products developed in the past four years. Innovation is their core competency.

Artificial intelligence is here and is most likely coming to your industry. Robots already used in manufacturing and logistics facilities will eventually be performing many tasks that humans currently perform.

The use of technology is the predominant way companies make process innovations. In Justin's landscaping business, for example, they've incorporated technology to improve hiring, job fit, hold team meetings, prepare estimates, communicate with customers, manage job schedules, and so much more. And he's keeping his eye on product innovations such as electric and solar-powered autonomous mowers, irrigation innovations that save water, and concrete pavers that reduce water runoff and waste.

### 3. BUSINESS MODEL INNOVATION

Business model innovation is when companies disrupt an entire industry. Examples include Uber, Lyft, and other ride-sharing companies that disrupted the taxi market; Airbnb and VRBO who disrupted the hotel and short-term rental markets; and Pandora, Spotify, and Napster who disrupted the music industry.

Now that you have some ideas about what types of innovations are available to you, let's look at what might make your products (and business) more valuable.

## GET YOURSELF READY TO GROW

I want to help your business to dominate your market. But I'm also there for you if you just want to create a sellable and sustainable company with a lasting enterprise value, even if it isn't the 800-pound gorilla topping everyone else in your field. Or maybe you're aiming for the kind of business that doesn't earn accolades but contends in any race or competition, making a go of it, supporting the family, enjoying the journey. Whichever category you're in, this book is for you.

Are you looking to improve your business? Are you ready to improve your life and the lives of those who work with and for you? Do you want to capitalize on the full potential of your people and opportunities? Are you ready to innovate by looking outside your own experience, business, and industry to find the best ways forward wherever they are?

The process of growing and expanding your business requires you to develop yourself. That means it's a path with many opportunities for fulfillment. But it also asks a lot of a person.

To get yourself ready to grow, you'll need to answer some basic questions.[8] (Don't worry if you don't have the answers to these questions just now. They will unfold over time—and this book will help.) But be thinking about:

How comfortable are you with risk? Are you confident you can remain profitable during growth?

Let's take this quick litmus test question: If I invested $1M in your business, how would you spend it? And what return on your money would you expect? Alternatively, if your company could borrow $1M at 6% interest, would you do it? Where would you invest this money?

If you are clear on your answers and can answer how you would grow the company, then you are on your way. Of course, you'll also need to answer other questions: How long do you plan to stay in business? How fast do you want to grow?

## TRANSITIONS REQUIRE LEADERSHIP DEVELOPMENT

To transfer your family's business from one generation to the next, the founder will need to empower you, the next-generation leader, to learn a new set of behaviors and skills while they let go of the reins.

To start, you need to make sure you are clean psychologically—meaning you are good with everyone in the family—especially if you are directly involved in the business. That said, there may be family members, such as siblings, not involved in the day-to-day management of the company; you will need to be clean with them, too.

Once the psychological rivalries are behind you, both the founder and the disruptive successor will need to identify gaps in talent, knowledge, or wisdom. You will need to understand what's available to be transferred from one generation to the next and what has to be acquired or learned from the outside.

As they adjust to new family and business dynamics, both

founders and next-generation leaders may want to search for some personal and professional development support from a leadership development program like this one, an executive coach, or even from a family psychologist.

## LEADERS NEED A PLAYBOOK

When a sports team is losing too many games, they fire their coach and hire a new one is hired. When that new coach starts, he should have a playbook that's going to improve the team; otherwise, he will likely go the way of the prior coach. But a playbook is only as good as the players using it. The players need to be coachable for the new coach's playbook to work. And the same is true of business leaders.

Players in sports need a playbook; so do leaders in business. And personal coaching usually helps, too. This book is your playbook, as you will see in the chapters to follow. Whether you choose to hire a coach is up to you. But you should know the benefits usually outweigh the investment, and the coach will get you further faster and shorten the road to your goal.

Having a business coach is not a sign of weakness. Instead, it's an expression of a desire to perform at an even higher level. Leaders who read books, learn from peers, and get regular coaching have demonstrated that they outperform leaders who don't do these things. A company's investment in providing coaching to its executives yields an average return on investment (ROI) of almost six times the cost of the coaching, according to *The Manchester Review* 2001.[9] Their study noted improvements in executive productivity, quality, customer service, retention, teamwork, supervisory relationships, working relationships among peers, and job satisfaction.

I see all this with my clients—along with increases in revenues, profitability, and business value.

## YOUR BIGGEST OBSTACLES ARE YOUR BLIND SPOTS

*"There are known knowns; there are things we know we know. We also know there are known unknowns; that is to say we know there are some things we do not know. But there are also unknown unknowns—the ones we don't know we don't know. And...it is the latter category that tend to be the difficult ones."*[10]

—DONALD RUMSFELD, FORMER US SECRETARY OF DEFENSE

There are things you know and things you don't know. Everyone has blind spots. The real danger is in not knowing what you don't know. Learn your blind spots, and your effectiveness as a leader will increase. Continue to be blind to them, and you're destined to derail yourself and those you lead.

Identifying and exploring your blind spots is one of the best ways to improve your effectiveness as a leader. The same goes for your team and each team member. Blind spots can cover capabilities, strengths, and weaknesses, and in every case, it is better to see them than to remain ignorant.

As your virtual coach for the duration of this book, I'm here to help you spot them—then improve on those areas.

Here are a few familiar "blind spot" areas you might see in yourself:

- **Overestimating your strategic capabilities:** Are you a leader with a strong operational background? Do you often think you "know it all" because you are a better operator than others in your industry? If so, you might overestimate your ability to incorporate big-picture/strategic thinking or your ability to close the gap between your present state of business and your future desired state. Because you execute plans better than most, you overestimate what your team can do and most likely underestimate the importance of strategy.

- **Not being coachable:** When a leader thinks they already "know it all," they value being right. Therefore, they are unwilling to spend much time listening to others. These people may appear invulnerable and not open to feedback. They may interrupt people and end conversations abruptly, signaling to followers that it's a waste of time to raise contrary opinions and ideas.
- **Believing the rules don't apply to you:** At some point, many leaders develop a sense of entitlement along with their success, power, and authority. A leader with this flaw might not think that the same rules apply to them as apply to everyone else.

In my experience, leaders who aren't aware of their blind spots or disregard them lead from a dangerous place. At one extreme, they can be dangerously ineffective, and at the other, they can be dangerously toxic.

## ONLY COACH THE COACHABLE

I have one cardinal rule in my coaching practice: Only coach the coachable. These are the people who are young enough in their hearts and minds to be learners.

So my question to you as you continue to read on is, are you a learner? Because it's your mindset and passion that will determine whether this book is going to be useful to you—the same things that will likely determine your business success. If this book is to help you through your issues in your family business, then you'll need to be coachable while you read it.

Below is a list of questions to which mostly YES answers mean you are coachable:

1. Are you approachable?
2. Are you receptive?
3. Are you curious?
4. Are you humble?
5. Are you trusting?
6. Are you open to new possibilities?
7. Can you be objective?
8. Do you listen with the intent to learn?
9. Can you listen without being defensive?
10. Can you listen without saying, "I know that"?
11. Do you regularly ask others for feedback or criticism?
12. Do you invest in your professional development?

I have heard many people in years past say things like, "I don't have the time right now," or "Let's talk after I hire my assistant," or "I need to resolve some things first." What they're really saying is, "Now isn't the right time for me to work on improving my foundational business skills and processes." But only on rare occasions have I seen any benefits of waiting. Things don't just get better after you hire a second in command, or you find someone to head up the selling and marketing of your business, or you put new software into place, or you deal with some family issues. Some of these sound like legitimate reasons because coaching can be time-consuming, and there is often a bit of an up-front time investment curve in learning. But most of the time, waiting is a diversion from taking action and getting the help you need. The truth is that there is never an ideal time to start coaching, and there will always be an excuse to hold off and wait for a better time.

That's why, in this book, I'm going to you some of my best coaching advice without you ever having to work directly with me. If you are coachable, ready to be coached, and want to grow, then let's move on to what you need to do, like implementing the 7 P's Playbook in your business.

If you are not coachable, then why bother reading any more of this book? There are many more enjoyable books of fiction, not to mention articles on current events, politics, or sports. You can read those if you just want to pass the time enjoyably; this is a book about implementing what you are learning.

## FORM FIRST, FUNCTION SECOND

I've seen the tools of tools in my business and in my clients' businesses. I have seen firsthand how the skilled use of the right tool changes a leader's way of thinking. I have witnessed many times how effective my clients become after they incorporate one of our business growth tools into their thinking.

For example, many prospective clients complain before working with me that their people are unaccountable to what's vital in their business. The question I am quick to ask is, "So what are the priorities of the business and their department or role?" They usually say, "Well..." and then drift off into some long-winded admission that priorities are not established or communicated.

When thinking about your business, it's vital that you figure out the form first and the functions second. When thinking about your organizational needs, it's best to think in terms of organizational structure: what does the organization ideally look like? Most people, however, usually start with the organizational chart, which is about what the organization currently looks like.

Next, you should define your company's functions—for example, sales, operations, finance, and then the roles within each function. Too many business owners start by placing themselves and their people on their organizational chart, then later try to describe all the things that a specific person does for the company. This approach prioritizes the person over the function and the function over the form (structure) when it should be the other way around. Form first; function second; person third.

Similarly, when it comes to learning how to scale up while navigating the intergenerational transfer of a family business, I present you the form (framework) first and the function (tools) second. That is, we'll start with the 7 P's, then cover the growth tools in the chapters devoted to each of those P's.

## THE 7 P'S PLAYBOOK

Many small businesses, especially family-run businesses, operate informally—that is, without a business playbook that describes the management structure. A good playbook creates an organizational environment where teammates collaborate to achieve common goals. It provides clear functional responsibilities and has consistent language for the activities, systems, and processes of the business.

In the absence of systems managed by excellent or above-average employees, the owners become the system. They depend on nobody but close family members and key employees who, through many years of hard work and devotion, have earned the respect of the owners. But if you are going to scale up your business or build a company that is worth a fortune when you sell it, you will have to make sure it is not too dependent on you or any key employees.

I designed the 7 P's Playbook, and its corresponding set of tools, to provide an understanding of the role you, the entrepreneur, play in managing your business. Let's briefly go through each element of the playbook. By the time you finish reading this book, you should be able to apply the tools that belong to each of the 7 P's to your business.

In a family business, if you are going to disrupt your successor and build a company with 5–10x the current revenues, profits, and enterprise value, you need to follow these seven plays in my playbook:

1. Redefine Your **Purpose**
2. **Plan** for Your 10x
3. Redefine Your **Products**
4. Develop Your **People** into A-Players
5. Set Your **Priorities**
6. Build Out Your **Processes**
7. Measure Your **Performance**

## PURPOSE

Most business leaders say that to drive success and motivate people, you need a big why. That means you need to be clear on your reason for being, your cause, your belief that something would be missing in the world if you went away. Your purpose lays the foundation for why you're doing what you're doing. It's different from the founder's purpose (which may have been to make a living to support the family).

Another reason to have a clearly defined purpose is to attract top talent. If your vision is to make yourself wealthy, that might inspire you personally, but it's not going to encourage the other people you will need on your team. Talented people want to join a winning team that is heading someplace significant. If your vision/purpose is a big one, others can see themselves achieving what they hope to accomplish in life within the scope of your company's mission. A poorly defined, small, or uninspiring purpose is almost worse than not having one.

As a disruptive successor, you will likely need to reestablish and redefine your company's why. That's because your founders' why isn't yours. If you want people to follow you as you begin leading the company, you'll need to engage them on an emotional level, touching their hearts with your sincerity, passion, and purpose.

## PLAN

Imagine for a moment that you are building a 5,000-square-foot home on land you own. When you arrive on the building site, you see workers scrambling around doing work, but everyone seems to be working randomly. When you ask the general contractor to show you the blueprints, they say, "We decided not to use blueprints. We're just winging it, and we'll see what happens." Would you keep them on as your general contractor? Of course you wouldn't, but how many business owners and leaders go to work each day without a clear plan?

The fact is, you cannot scale a business without a plan and a team aligned around it. And you will not get buy-in from investors, employees, or customers if you have not communicated essential elements of your intention to them. People follow leaders with visions. And without plans, visions are nothing but hallucinations.

If you are a disruptive successor, your vision and plan need to reflect your desire to achieve significant growth and your ability to innovate and improve the current state of the business.

## PRODUCTS

What is your product/service? What does your brand represent? What makes your product different from other products/services? What are the market conditions that make it useful to the people or companies who buy it?

Building excellence and differentiation into your product/service is vital to building value in your business. Mastering your product/service has to be coupled with learning how to differentiate it in the marketplace. Having a better product/service by itself doesn't guarantee anything; in fact, it's often not the best product that dominates a market but the best-marketed one. As a disruptive successor, to increase your company's value, you may need to overhaul the product/service, as well as how you produce it, deliver it, position it, and sell it to improve your competitive advantage.

## PEOPLE

You, your people, and your leadership of them are the most critical ingredients in the success of your business. I cannot stress it enough that attracting, recruiting, interviewing, selecting, hiring, onboarding, training, coaching, motivating, and managing people is vital to your success. Leading and managing are critical, as is building a cohesive team. Ultimately, the people you hire to grow your business and execute your plan are what matter the most in any venture. If you don't have the right people, then you cannot execute well on any strategy.

Building a high-performing culture in your business not only requires amazing people; it also requires building a culture that maximizes the effects of your high-potential people.

It's more than likely that some favorite employees who worked well under your parent's management will have to adjust to a new leader, new processes, and growth. You may need to have some difficult conversations with these employees, as they will have to change for the business to grow.

## PRIORITIES

To execute a plan, you need objectives, desired results, data/metrics, communication, meetings to manage communication flow, clear accountabilities, and the ability to manage the time and priorities of yourself and others.

In the chapters on priorities, I'll discuss all of these vital interlocking elements and the important role meetings play to keep your priorities on track. Many small businesses have been successful for years without shared awareness of company financials, company goals, and priorities. The days of command-and-control leadership have given way to the shared leadership, ownership, and transparency that comes from having a next-generation leader.

## PROCESSES

A good organization is built upon a set of methods that are thorough and comprehensive to make up an entire system. A well-organized business, therefore, is a system of systems. To create a valuable and sellable business that can run in your absence requires great systems managed by people with above-average talent.

As the family business grows to include more people, you can no longer rely on conversations around the family dinner table to get things done. By developing standard processes, you can create a business that any qualified individual, not just a family member, can run.

### PERFORMANCE

Profitability, critical financial ratios such as return on capital, and KPIs (key performance indicators) are all measures of how well your company is performing. Plenty of small businesses roll on with an incomplete understanding of how to use these measures. That may be fine in the short term, but it's not going to support healthy growth.

Your company is growing, and you need to run it accordingly. Professionally run companies report financial results to shareholders in a meaningful manner. Disruptive successors, especially from the millennial generation, share financial information more freely than their parents did. But before you can do that effectively, you must understand the data so you can present it correctly.

The 7 P's form a circular playbook; you could begin at any P, because the playbook builds on itself like a flywheel. But the best way to start is to consider why you are in the business you are in, and so, we begin with Purpose.

CHAPTER 2

# PURPOSE

## WHAT IS YOUR WHY?

*"People don't buy what you do; they buy why you do it. And what you do simply proves what you believe."*

—SIMON SINEK, BRITISH-AMERICAN AUTHOR AND MOTIVATIONAL SPEAKER

What was it that inspired your parents or their parents to start this business? It was probably something well beyond making a profit or supporting the family. I know that making money is an important motivator. I've heard it many times before: "Well, I had a new child on the way, so I needed to buckle down and get serious so that I could provide for my family." I always push back on them and ask, "But why *this* business? Why *this* industry? You could have picked any number of other businesses or industries, yet you chose this one. Why?"

The answer is simple yet difficult to answer. Like so many of us who lead unexamined lives, perhaps they just fell into the business. Or maybe they had what Michael Gerber, author of The E-Myth, called an "entrepreneurial seizure." That is, they woke up one day asking themselves, "Why am I working for this boss when I could work for myself?" Or perhaps they took over someone else's business. Maybe they bought into the founder's vision, even if it wasn't clearly defined.

Believe it or not, it matters how and why you came to be in the business you're in. And you'll need to examine whether the founder's reason for getting into the business is the same as yours. Otherwise, you need to reevaluate based on your why.

The reason this matters is that the people you are leading want to know your why before they follow you. If you are a disruptive successor, your why is going to be bigger and probably more badass than that of your parent(s). And you need to figure it out to create the followership you want from your leaders, managers, and employees.

## WRIGHT VERSUS LANGLEY

Let's take the story of Samuel Pierpont Langley and compare it to that of Orville and Wilbur Wright. In 1900, both Langley and the Wright brothers were in pursuit of the same objective: invent human-crewed flight.

Samuel Pierpont Langley was a highly educated and esteemed scientist and secretary of the Smithsonian Institution who worked with enormous government support and public exposure. Langley had all the resources—money, fame, and publicity—while the Wright brothers had none of those things. Orville and Wilbur Wright were the owners of a bicycle shop who worked hard using their limited resources. Langley's launch amid lots of fanfare failed, while nine days later, the Wright brothers took flight quietly. The point of the story is that Langley's purpose was to seek fame and fortune whereas the Wright brothers were driven to invent and experiment.

## WHAT BUSINESS ARE YOU REALLY IN AND WHY?

Your reason for being in business matters because people want to work for an inspired leader with a vision. So what business are you really in? The answer is usually anything but obvious. That's because you often have some hidden cause, mission, or motive such as wanting to change the way business is conducted in your industry. You want to set a new standard. You see a better way.

If you want people to follow you as you build a lasting business, you need to find a purpose and communicate it to those around you.

B. C. Forbes, the founder of *Forbes* magazine, once said, "Don't forget until too late that the business of life is not business but living." Wouldn't that suggest there is a higher purpose than making a profit?

Peter Drucker, one of the most widely known and influential thinkers on modern management, whose work continues to be used by managers worldwide, described purpose this way:

> *The mission (purpose) statement is the foundation for priorities, strategies, plans, and work assignments. It is the starting point for the design of managerial jobs and, above all, for the design of managerial structures. Nothing may seem simpler or more obvious than to know what a company's business is...Actually, "What is our business" is almost always a difficult question, and the right answer is usually anything but obvious.*[11]

In my opinion, especially for family businesses, business is your way of life. It's how you communicate and relate to each other, and at home, it's often the subject of common interest and understanding.

We are all engaged in business. The question is how we relate to the why of being in business. Is your business a vehicle for accomplishing something for you to explore something else you are passionate about, such as art, family, innovation, human potential, philanthropy, or community service? Is your purpose to serve others? To search for knowledge and truth? To pursue beauty and excellence? To change the world?

Trust me, there's a lot more than just making money. Making money is a necessary by-product of the work we do. You'll need to dig deep to find your why, and you'll need to ask the founder what their original passion or purpose was when they started the company.

Need I say more? You must find your why. After all, it engages team members emotionally, causing them to work around and through obstacles, and inspires change—permanent, lasting change.

## RAISING THE BAR

When Justin took on the role of CEO, he knew he wanted to grow the business significantly beyond what his parents had accomplished. He probably knew that he had to evaluate his purpose against his father's intention if he was going to get people to follow him. And as his coach, I was there to identify what obstacles might be in his way to scaling up the business.

If he had stuck with the why that his father had, his business would not have scaled up as it has during these past several years.

Kendel White founded the business decades earlier after a stint as a chef in a restaurant. He decided he could make more money as a landscaper running his own business. His purpose was to support his family by doing something he enjoyed and was good at. The business grew to a modest $1.5M-per-year company and met the needs of himself, his family, and their small staff of ten to fifteen employees.

But Justin, who grew up in the business, had other interests by the time he took it over. He has a keen mind for business and a passion for leadership and community involvement. To grow this business, he had to identify his purpose and recruit many new employees. At first, when I took him through business coaching exercises about purpose, he thought his company's mission might be to provide a path for immigrants to citizenship. But after more profound thought, his aim was revealed to him more clearly.

His purpose was to "raise the bar" in his business, in the landscape industry, and in his community. By raising the bar, he could achieve the mission of improving the lives of those who joined his company.

Today, everything in their business is evaluated against its purpose. They evaluate prospective employees based on whether they buy into the purpose. They are leaders in their local community and the landscape industry through the statewide association. Their fleet of vehicles, uniformed employees, marketing messages and materials, and monthly pro bono community projects are all ways of expressing their leadership and raising the bar in the landscape industry.

So are they in the landscape business? Or are they in the business of elevating their people, their processes, their profits and the industry at large?

## SIMON SINEK'S GOLDEN CIRCLE: WHAT, HOW, WHY

Companies that are built to last have a strong core and a compelling purpose. Take Apple, one of the most successful companies on the planet.

In Simon Sinek's 2009 TED Talk—the most-watched TED

Talk of all time as of my writing this—he explains the power and popularity of Apple products. In his speech, he contrasts Dell, Gateway, and Apple, who at the time all competed in the same market for computers, monitors, and MP3 players. So why did people favor Apple over Dell and Gateway? It's because customers were passionate about Apple as a company. Apple has always been about delivering imaginative and attractive products that are simply designed *and* challenge the status quo! As a result, it built a loyal following.

After all, Steve Jobs's mission statement for Apple in 1980, according to *The Economist*, was, "To contribute to the world by making tools for the mind that advance humankind." That's what differentiated them from their competitors.

When a company is living its purpose, the business they are in becomes secondary to their why.

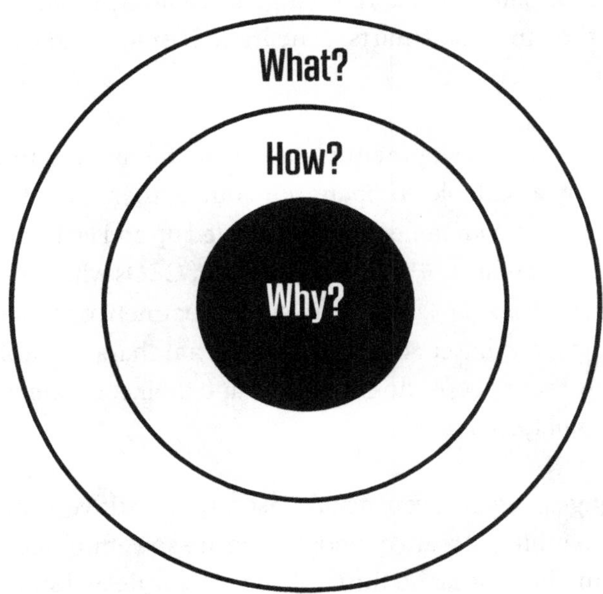

## FIND YOUR WHY TO CREATE YOUR FOLLOWERSHIP

If you want to build a multigenerational business that lasts and inspires people to follow you, you'll probably need to either reinvigorate the founder's purpose or invent your own. First, you'll have to gain the trust of those employees who are older than you and were hired by your parents. They might think you seem entitled because you inherited the business. So you'll need to prove to them otherwise. You will need to touch their hearts with *your* message. To reach their hearts, you need to be a caring person with competence and character. If you connect with only their minds, they may find reasons to disagree with you over time. But if you reach both their hearts and their minds, they will respect and adore you.

Once you build a team of followers, then you want to develop them into leaders who, like you, are training, coaching, and educating others. They, too, will need to become leaders of character, empathy, and intelligence. And by intelligence, I don't mean book smarts. I mean high emotional quotient (EQ).

Leadership development is one of the talents required for building a scalable company. Of course, there are plenty of examples of companies that have scaled up and lack people of character at the top. There are stories of CEOs who were fired because of sexual harassment, unfair treatment of employees, arduous working conditions, and immoral character. Still, ultimately these people do get ousted, and their companies most often fall from grace.

Scaling up requires you to build lasting competitive advantage by assembling a team of people who are so committed to the dream, the cause, and the work that very little will stop them.

Did you ever try to stop someone passionate about what they were doing? No, because there is no stopping them. They work long hours to do what they believe serves their purpose. That's why people are your most significant competitive advantage. Get your people right, and you will get the right things done.

*"If you hire people just because they can do a job, they'll work for your money. But if you hire people who believe what you believe, they'll work for you with blood and sweat and tears."*

—SIMON SINEK

## CRAFTING YOUR VISION IS POWERFUL

In their book *Built to Last: Successful Habits of Visionary Companies*, Jim Collins and Jerry Porras provided some of the best research on this subject. Their research supports the fact that companies built to last are built upon grand, expansive visions. They coined the term BHAG® (Big Hairy Audacious Goal) to label this feature—having a huge ten- to twenty-five-year goal—common to great companies.

So why are visions so powerful?

Grand visions change attitudes and inspire action. They keep people focused and aligned around the target, the strategy, and the plan to get there. A compelling vision is practical and serves as a guide for setting priorities and objectives, making decisions, and evaluating progress toward goals.

What defines effective vision statements? They are future focused and provide a big picture of what the organization will look like in a few years. They are also directional, meaning they guide the organization's plans and strategies. They are specific and focused enough to shape decision making. They are relevant and purpose driven, and they reflect companies' responses to the challenges of the day.

Effective vision statements share the following common characteristics. They are:

- Imaginable
- Desirable
- Feasible
- Focused
- Flexible
- Communicable

## POWERFUL VISION STATEMENTS

There are many good examples of vision statements that have become recognizable because they got great companies to great heights. Keep in mind that these are just a starting point. The vision behind these statements is much more robust and comprehensive.

Below are a few examples:

> **Amazon's** vision is to be Earth's most customer-centric company, to build a place where people can come to find and discover anything they might want to buy online.

> **General Electric's** vision is to become the world's premier digital industrial company, transforming industry with software-defined machines and solutions that are connected, responsive, and predictive.

**Southwest Airlines'** vision is "To become the world's most loved, most flown, and most profitable airline."

**Whole Foods Market's** vision statement is synonymous with its motto: "Whole Foods, Whole People, Whole Planet." In expanded form, the company's vision statement is as follows: "Our motto—'Whole Foods, Whole People and Whole Planet'—emphasizes that our vision reaches far beyond just being a food retailer. Our success in fulfilling our vision is measured by customer satisfaction, team member excellence and happiness, return on capital investment, improvement in the state of the environment, and local and larger community support. Our ability to instill a clear sense of interdependence among our various stakeholders (the people who are interested and benefit from the success of our company) is contingent upon our efforts to communicate more often, more openly, and more compassionately. Better communication equals better understanding and more trust."

**IKEA's** vision is "To create a better everyday life for the many people," and their business idea is "To offer a wide range of well-designed, functional home furnishing products at prices so low that as many people as possible will be able to afford them."

**Nike's** vision is "To bring inspiration and innovation to every athlete in the world," while its mission statement is to "do everything possible to expand human potential."

**Zappos's** vision is "Delivering happiness to customers, employees, and vendors." And their mission statement is to "provide the best customer service possible. Deliver WOW through service."

I find the vision statements of my clients to be among the most inspiring, perhaps because I played a part in creating them and seeing to their accomplishment.

My clients' vision statements are one-page documents that outline short- and long-term plans and company strategy. They include corporate values that reflect what they believe in and how they do business—for example, "customer first." They challenge and inspire members of the team to do great things and raise their standards. They identify the ninety-day and one-year goals along the path to the three- to five-year and ten- to twenty-five-year goals. They highlight what makes their organization different and why their business matters. Finally, the vision statements inspire the stakeholders (employees and shareholders first), and demonstrate that the company is committed to a cause beyond just making a profit.

Purpose (or mission) statements are a must because they give everyone a reason to show up. Core values form the cultural norms and standards of behavior at the company and can make the entire workforce aspire to a higher purpose. Consider the technology company I discussed earlier that is disrupting the retail experience in the furniture industry. Their purpose is "changing the retail shopping experience," which is compelling enough to inspire people to do work that is above and beyond the industry norm. Their purpose is just one small element of their vision document, but it's the starting point because it's their reason for being.

K&D Landscaping Inc. brings its team together every quarter to update its vision and review the prior quarter's achievements. What drives them is their purpose of "raising the bar" in their industry. It infuses what they do. They hire people who embrace and live it. Company marketing and messaging reflects it, as does their commitment to giving back to the community and industry. And, of course, the appearance of their trucks and their job sites reflects it, too. Everything is done with the intent to "raise the bar."

## SO WHAT'S YOUR VISION?

Do you have prospective investors whom you need to get excited about the disruption you are making in the world? Have you thought up ways to sell your vision to your employees? Most of my clients use what many call the "all-hands company meeting" to convey that message. It's a speech that gets updated every quarter but repeated often enough that the message is never lost or forgotten.

For a vision to be active and alive in an organization, you and the other leaders need to sell it. You need to communicate your message to them often. Share the passion you feel for the business with them. Share your purpose. After all, you (or your parents or grandparents) are the founder; you need to ignite the passion in others.

Discuss strategy and goals with your people. Where are you going? What short- and long-term objectives do you have? What's in it for them if you achieve them? Emphasize how everyone will benefit from your success—a rising tide lifts all boats. Raise the bar in your business. Remember to sell the same vision in your marketing materials, on your website, in your sales calls, and your customer service and support calls.

But first, you'll have to give them a plan, or collaborate to develop a plan, which is the subject of the next chapter.

### ACTION STEPS

1. Download our why worksheet under the Resources/Tools section of the www.DisruptiveSuccessor.com website.
2. Develop your why: your purpose statement, your reason for being in business. You can't stay in business if you can't make a profit, but your why needs to be more than making a profit.
3. Share your why. Make sure the leaders on your team believe in it as much as you do.
4. You're now well on your way to creating a culture people want to belong to.

## CHAPTER 3

# PLAN

## STRATEGIZING FOR YOUR 10X

*"Good business leaders create a vision, articulate the vision, passionately own the vision, and relentlessly drive it to completion."*

—JACK WELCH

You need a creative vision to make a difference in the world. But vision alone is not enough; you also need execution. A Japanese proverb teaches, "Vision without action is a daydream. Action without vision is a nightmare."

Planning in a family business doesn't often happen in any formal way because family members believe they are in such frequent communication that their partners already know their thoughts about the business. But this is where many family founders are mistaken!

Planning requires you to slow down and confront the brutal facts about your family business: what's working well, what's not working so well, and what's broken. You must look at yourself, your people, and your processes. Then you must fix what's broken, improve what's not working so well, and leverage your strengths.

Planning forces you to take the time to reaffirm your vision and map out your priorities, goals, and targets. It gets you to adopt a more strategic focus, which should translate to earning more money and working effectively and efficiently so that you can enjoy the journey as you grow yourself, your team, and your business.

Strategic Planning, correctly parsed, becomes Strategic Thinking + Execution Planning.

To become an effective leader, you must learn to be highly productive so you can achieve exceptional results in the shortest possible period and with the least possible effort. When you are effective, you are focused on doing the right things. Only then can you accomplish a lot in a short period.

Many people often confuse the word effectiveness with the word efficiency, but they are very different from each other. *Effectiveness* is about **doing the right things** to produce superior results. *Efficiency* is about **doing things right** to deliver those results rapidly.

*"Management is doing things right; leadership is doing the right things."*

—PETER F. DRUCKER

In short, to be more productive, you must employ more leverage. And to be more strategic, which will produce the greatest results, you must plan and execute on the most important, highest priority and highest leverage activities.

## WHAT GOES INTO A PLAN?

A strategic plan or business plan, then, is a description of your business, why it exists, where it is going in the next ninety days, one year, three to five years, and possibly even ten years. It should include a description of the products/services and any unique promises of your brand, a description of your customers, the market your serve, and how you will market and deliver the products/services to your customers. And it should highlight what makes you different from your competitors. I call this your strategy. Your tactics define your immediate and longer-term priorities, goals, and measurable activities. Your key performance indicators (KPIs) or objectives and key results (OKRs) are the specific, measurable, attainable, relevant, and time-bound (SMART) goals that align with the company's strategy. These are the scorecard items to watch, measure, and manage.

In other words, your strategic plan includes a high-level overview of your company and its marketing, product/operations, and finances.

## STEP AWAY TO MAKE YOUR PLAN

If you or your parent started this business, there were probably some big ideas about how the company was going to look. Unfortunately, too many business owners don't quite realize their entrepreneurial dream and find themselves working too many hours for too little money. That's why you need to get away from the business to plan. It's just too difficult to create a compelling vision when you are caught up in the day-to-day.

So step away. Head to your thinking place for some strategy and execution planning, and the results will speak for themselves. You will see increased levels of engagement from your employees when you set monster-sized goals or involve them in a substantial change. You'll see an increased commitment to small actions, to weekly, monthly, and quarterly goals, and to annual initiatives meant to accomplish big things.

When you don't meet your commitments or goals—and there will be times when you cannot or do not—what will you do?

LEARN. We learn when we set goals and achieve them. We also learn when we set goals and don't achieve them. How does that saying go? "If at first you don't succeed, try, try again." So we try again. Eventually, we become so good at setting our vision and motivating others to reach the mountaintop that we drop the notion of "trying" and, as Nike says, "just do it."

Learning from mistakes is critical. Doing things differently and better next time is even more so.

As I like to say, what got you here won't get you there. The truth is that your mom, dad, or grandparents probably built a good business, maybe even a great business. But like most businesses, they didn't develop one that can withstand multiple generations.

To scale up your family business, you'll need clarity about where you're going, and you'll need a roadmap that you can share with all team members and shareholders. They need to know the plan and probably take part in developing it if they have the knowledge, skills, or insight to add value to that process. Developing this roadmap presents an opportunity to do some deep thinking. How often do you do that with your team or even alone? You'll need to get away to your thinking place where you can not only dare to dream, and dream BIG, but also document your dreams and vision.

You may want to hire a skilled facilitator, coach, or mentor who has the experience and know-how to guide the group. This person selects the appropriate business growth tools for the situation at hand and asks tough questions to challenge the team to work through any problematic dynamics.

The truth is, you probably respond to issues all day long and all week long, but this is not planning. Few people stop to assess where they are and where they're going. It's like looking from basecamp to the top of Mount Everest, a peak higher than you've ever reached before, and telling the team, "That is where we are going, and you should trust me as your leader to take you there."

Jonathan Swift, most famous as the author of *Gulliver's Travels*, said, "Vision is the art of seeing what is invisible to others."

Investors, shareholders, and stakeholders in the family business want to know where the business is going. And by stakeholders I mean anyone who has a vested interest in the company's success, which could include customers, employees, referral sources, vendors, and the like. The fact is that having a BIG vision, which stakeholders buy into, will drive the growth of the business.

## PLANNING GOES BEYOND PROFITS

There are other important topics to discuss in your planning session that go well beyond the financial results, which often are just lagging indicators of success.

These are things such as customer satisfaction, employee engagement, consistency and reliability of earnings such as might come from having long-term contracts or recurring revenue, and a leadership and management team that can run the business in the absence of the owner. These are leading indicators of success that go beyond the numbers and predict how the company will do in the future.

Leaders have a responsibility to manage and maneuver through market conditions such as seasonality, cyclicality, and economic downturns and upturns. All of these forces can be too much for the young, unseasoned, or arrogant leader. But the leader with humility, intuition, a thirst for knowledge, and structured thinking about market conditions is one a parent or founder can feel confident will make all the difference.

Another important force is, of course, the competition in the market, and any changes or trends in political, legal, regulatory, economic, social, technological, or international factors in the market.

Here, I have found the application of several structured thinking processes to be helpful:

- SWOT (Strengths, Weaknesses, Opportunities, and Threats). Strengths and weaknesses are internal to your company, so you have some control over them, whereas opportunities and threats are external to your company and must be exploited or protected against, respectively.
- Harvard Business School professor Michael Porter's Five Forces Analysis. This analysis looks at the threats from new entrants, substitute products, the negotiating power of buyers, and the bargaining power of suppliers along with rivalry among competitors.

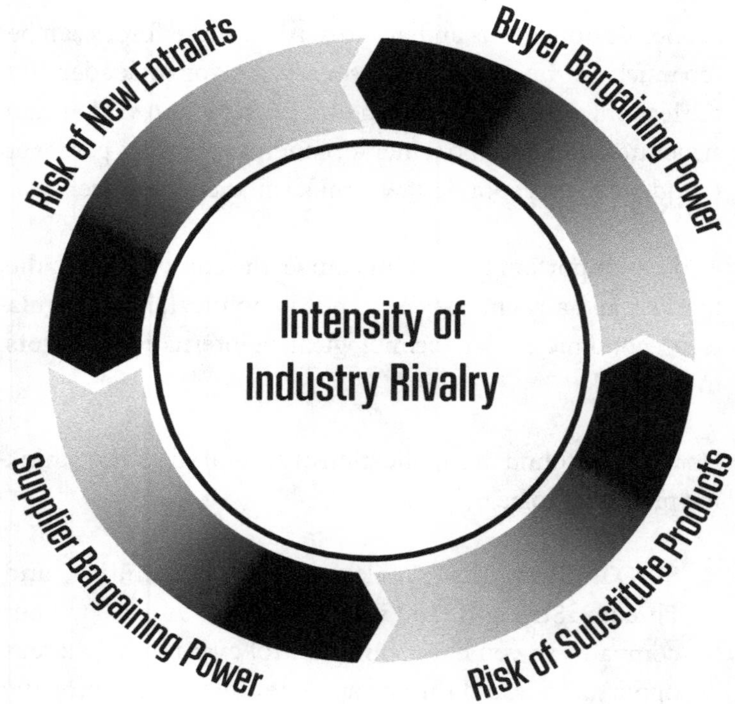


## WHEN YOU SHOULD CONSIDER A RETREAT

Hopefully, by now it is clear that getting away to plan out the company's next ninety days, next year, and next three to five years can clarify your strategic direction and tactics. If not, here are several more reasons to consider retreating to an off-site location to work on your business.

When everyone is in firefighting mode, it keeps you from working on the things that matter most. Occasionally, this will look like turf wars, silos, and politics within and between departments. Or perhaps the lines of communication are stopped up and nobody is sharing for the good of the company.

Planning is a great way to build consensus around a change in direction, to discuss a new project, or brainstorm a new product or repositioned service. Planning should result in an increase in top-line revenues; improvement in profitability; alignment of the entire company around key issues, challenges, and opportunities; and focus on the vital few activities to move the company forward.

## PREPARING FOR A PLANNING SESSION

Preparing for the retreat requires that you consider the purpose of your session.

What problems are you trying to solve? What work product or deliverable is expected as an outcome of the session—that is, what does success look like?

Who should attend the session? What are their perspectives or concerns? Will everyone attending be in favor of attending? Will all the attendees be on favorable terms with each other? If not, what must be done to deal with any conflict in the room?

What are the topics that should be covered in the room? What challenges or problems may arise? What prework, reading, learning, assessments, conversations, surveys, or analyses are needed to prepare for the discussions?

What is the agenda of the meeting? Where will the meeting be held, and what other logistics should be planned for? What is needed to facilitate conversation and record the decisions and actions to be taken next?

## A QUARTERLY RHYTHM

Everyone seems to agree that there is a natural rhythm to planning and that planning meetings should take place on a ninety-day cycle. This is a sufficient interval to act on goals, assess progress, and adopt more effective approaches, habits, and strategies. Of course, you will also need to meet weekly and monthly to evaluate your efforts against your plan and make sure you're getting your desired outcomes.

### ACTION STEPS

1. Visit the Resources section of my website, www.DisruptiveSuccessor.com, and download *How to Complete Our One-Page Strategic Plan* and *Strategic Planning: Preparing and Leading the Planning Process.*
2. Take some time to get away from your business. Seek out a place free of distractions where you can focus on your vision for the company. Decide whether you will hire a facilitator to set up and lead the meeting.
3. Answer some initial questions. Use the "reporter's questions" or "5 W's and H" (Who, What, Where, When, Why, and How) method. Answer these questions for your customers, products/services, employees, processes, priorities, and so on. For example: Who are your customers? What does your organization sell? When you take your business to the next level, what will it look like? Why are you in this business? How will you delight your customers, employees, and shareholders?

# CHAPTER 4

# PRODUCTS

## MARKETING VERSUS SELLING

*"Nothing happens until somebody sells something," and..."the fact is, everybody (vice presidents, operations managers, HR directors, IT people, customer service representatives, marketing people, accounting people, receptionists...everybody) can stay at home until somebody makes a sale."*

—PETER F. DRUCKER, MODERN MANAGEMENT THINKER

Your product is everything when you're running a small business, especially a family business. And your product is nothing without marketing and selling. If you don't improve your marketing and selling, you could fall into the 70% that fail, and if you fail to grow your top-line revenues (along with gross and net profit figures), the value of your business will not increase.

Now, I assume you already know on a fundamental level how to market and sell your products/services. (Note: Going forward, I use the word product when I mean product or service; in a service business, your service IS your product.) After all, you've gotten this far, so you've already figured out how to sustain your company. Most smaller family businesses market themselves to the public as a family business, thinking that this matters to their customers. But a disruptive successor in a family business knows that although this may be valuable to some customers, it's not relevant to all of them. I assume that as a disruptive successor, you want to have a high-growth firm, which is a business with ten or more employees that grows either its employees or revenues by an average of more than 20% per year for three consecutive years.[12]

But let me ask you a few questions:

- Do you have a strategy that differentiates you in the market?

- Is it resulting in the growth of your top-line revenues?
- Does your marketing support the efforts of your selling?

In this chapter, I'm going to teach you how to look at your marketing and sales in ways you may never have thought of before. But first, let's clarify the difference between marketing and selling.

Simply stated:

- Marketing is a one-to-many education.
- Selling is one-to-one persuasion.
- Marketing is responsible for generating qualified leads or lead generation.
- Selling is responsible for converting those leads into customers or lead conversion.

**Short story longer,** marketing, as defined by the American Marketing Association (AMA), is "the activity, set of institutions, and processes for creating, communicating, delivering, and exchanging offerings that have value for customers, clients, partners, and society at large." In other words, marketing is about educating your target market on how your product/service will satisfy their needs and wants. It has less to do with getting customers to pay for your product as it does with developing demand for a product that fills the customer's needs.

Think of it like this. Marketing is the air war support to selling, which is the ground war. Selling is turning a prospective customer from a contact into a contract. AMA defines personal selling as oral presentation in a conversation with one or more potential purchasers to make a sale; it is the ability to persuade people to buy goods and services at a profit to the seller and benefit to the buyer.

## MARKETING BASICS

The essential elements of marketing are market, market research, message, and medium.

The *market*, sometimes called your sandbox or target market, defines the attributes of your target customer. These might include demographics, geographics, sociographics, or distribution (selling) channels. And your market might have one to three avatars or ideal client profiles. For example, my target market is closely held and family-owned businesses that are growing. And my perfect client is the next-generation leader, typically a millennial, in a family business with 10 to 250 employees, who is looking to upgrade their leadership and dramatically scale their business.

*Market research* is the process of gathering information about your customers' needs and preferences. It helps you understand who your customer is, what they want, where they live, where they work, and how to reach them. Here, you are considering their demographics, psychographics, and sociographics. Market research is usually needed to define your core customer or ideal customer—that is, the customer you think about when you develop your messaging.

The *message* is what you are communicating to your market. It should embody your unique value proposition or unique selling position and thus improve your positioning in the market. The message ideally generates awareness and stimulates demand from the right type of customer.

The *medium* is your go-to-market strategy, more specifically the channels you use to promote your offerings—for example, social media, direct mail, television, radio, newspaper advertising, and so forth.

To manage the marketing spend and measure its effectiveness, you should have a marketing budget, calendar, and some type of lead tracking system.

## SELLING BASICS

For salespeople to be effective at converting leads into sales, your marketing must educate prospective customers in support of your salespeople's efforts. Otherwise, all the marketing and selling will fall to the salesperson, making their job twice as tough. Your salespeople will benefit from a defined sales process to make selling more natural and not put extra burden on them. They will benefit from training on sales scripts and improvisation practice to help them sound natural rather than scripted. Typically, this type of training teaches them how to take the prospective customer through a journey and with such enthusiasm that the customer wants to refer others to do business with the company.

The typical journey through your sales process starts with some rapport building. Next, you'll want to establish why the prospective customer is speaking with you—that is, what are their needs/wants, their pain/frustration in their current situation, or the pleasure they hope to gain? You'll want to clarify their budget—probing for something definitive—and identify who else might be involved in the decision. Only then, after you have gathered all this information, will you drive toward a closed sale or commitment to the next step.

If you have the right salespeople, then they'll always be

improving on their selling behaviors, attitudes, and skills such as listening, presenting, storytelling, and problem solving.

Selling gets more complex, of course, when you are selling an intangible service, a more expensive product or service, or something that requires more marketing education from both buyers and sellers.

## DO YOU NEED A MARKETING PLAN?

Unless you have a steady stream of leads contacting, you need a marketing plan if you want to increase income and profits. Actively managing and focusing your marketing will get you better quality leads at a lower cost per lead. Otherwise, you have no roadmap. So unless the business is just rolling in the door, get to work on your marketing plan.

Part science, part art, and developed with lots of hunches and experimentation, good marketing plans have several standard features:

**Research:** You need to make sure you understand the needs and wants of your customers, especially your ideal ones. What are their frustrations? Pain points? What problem of theirs do you solve? What desires do you satisfy? You can gather this information from your customers directly or from secondary sources such as trade magazines. Typically, collecting it firsthand from your customers is the best.

**Target Market:** You can make assumptions about your customers, but it's better to collect information from them firsthand. This is called primary research. Secondary research is data collected from other sources such as newspapers, magazines, and studies. If you want to know who your customers are, spend time getting to know them. Focus on your best customers, your ideal or core customers, the ones who buy your product/service in the quantity required for you to make an optimal profit. You should be able to develop an ideal client/customer profile or buyer persona that has both demographic (age, gender, income, etc.) and psychographic (interests, attitudes, etc.) information. Once you understand who your ideal customer is, you want to speak to them in your messaging.

**Competitive Analysis and Positioning:** You need to know whom you are competing against and what they are offering so that you can communicate your message differently. The problem with most marketing is that companies fail to describe what is unique about their company. Prospective customers thus default to comparing based on price. A differentiator is your unique value proposition (UVP). It's also called your unique selling position (USP). Once you identify it, your job is to create a marketing program that communicates it to your target audience, which requires some imagination. It's challenging and may require going through a guided process to develop your positioning, message, and creative acts. I will cover this in more depth in the section on positioning.

I use several marketing exercises to help clients develop this understanding. The activities are designed to challenge clients to think about who their core customer is, what makes their marketing different from competitors', and how to position and tell their story.

Examples of questions are:

1. Who is your ideal client?

2. Do you know which of your core products generate the most gross profit dollars?
3. Do you have any key search words or phrases that place you first in an online search?
4. What unique promises or guarantees are there behind your business or branded products?
5. Are there any mechanisms you have in place that act as catalysts to spur purchasing?
6. Can you simply state what is different about your product from competitors' products?
   A. Do you deliver your services differently from competitors?
   B. What other activities differentiate you from the competition?

**Your Go-to-Market Strategy:** Every company has a way they go to market. For example, the founder of a new salsa recipe may do so by selling her products at the local farmers market. A janitorial services company may go to market by taking property managers of commercial buildings out to lunch. A plumbing business might have internet advertising on Yelp or Google as their go-to-market strategy.

Successful companies like yours probably have several channels through which to promote your business. You may rely on customer referrals, referrals from strategic partners, social media marketing, local advertising, trade shows, direct mail, or cold calls to targeted customers. If you can keep track of where your leads are coming from, you can focus on the activities that work and invest more time, money, and energy into them, while letting the other methods drop off.

**Pricing:** In this section of your plan, you will describe your pricing strategy. You could be priced to be premium price, market competitive price, low price, or lowest price. Most of my clients are in the premium to market competitive range, based on some combination of costs plus markup and market price. I have never had a client whose ambition was to be the low-price leader because it requires superior operational effectiveness to be a leader on price.

**Promotions:** Discounting, trials, and promotions play a prominent role in many businesses' success. Promotions timed to keep sales going during slow seasons or to incentivize customers to purchase, as well as upsells to get people to buy a more expensive product can make sense for the right business. When, if ever, do these come into effect? I don't recommend discounting without a corresponding reduction in value. But if you are in a retail business or price-competitive business, you probably need to consider this approach to generate cash flow.

**Budget:** If we're going to keep track of which marketing methods are most effective, we need to set a budget for each of our go-to-market strategies and the supporting materials and research they each require. An overall budget that is pegged to your total revenue needs to be reviewed. Overspending and underspending on marketing are two of the biggest mistakes I commonly see. Unfortunately, you can't know whether you are overspending or underspending until you test different activities. What works one day may stop working the next. It can be a guessing game, and the effectiveness of your marketing can be difficult to measure. Nonetheless, we need to try to measure against some goals based on experience and modify and review periodically.

**Metrics:** Any good marketing program measures its effectiveness wherever possible. If you can, you should keep track of the sources of leads, the number of leads and cost to generate them, the cost to acquire a customer, the average size of a transaction, the lifetime value of a customer, the churn (or turnover) of customers, and more. These are measures that you should maintain over time to see trends and changes.

**Sales Plan:** To convert your targeted leads into customers or clients, you'll want a sales plan that covers elements not covered in your marketing plan, such as prospecting, your sales process, your team, their tools, their metrics, and their targets/goals. Leads generated from one-to-one networking, referrals, business friends, and strategic partners are the responsibility of salespeople. They need a process to take them from contact to contract. Having a well-defined selling process will help create standardization among salespeople selling similar products/services, provide a teachable process for salespeople, and ensure that you are offering something that meets the needs of customers. If the sales process is teachable, valuable to customers, and repeatable, it's easily scalable.

Other issues to consider are: Who is on the sales team? How many people will you need? What tools and software and training resources will they need to do their job? Examples of goals are revenue targets, number of units sold, frequency of transactions, and conversion rates. What are the goals for each person and the team?

## FIVE WAYS TO GROW ANY BUSINESS'S SALES

There are five levers to grow any business. If you improve one or two of these, your revenues will increase geometrically, but if you improve several at once, your revenues will increase exponentially.

THE FIVE LEVERS ARE:

1. Leads generated (typically a marketing function)
2. Leads converted (a sales function)
3. Conversion ratio (the ratio of leads converted to leads generated)
4. Average size sale (increased by upselling to a more expensive purchase or cross-selling other products/services)
5. Repeat business or frequency

Companies whose business models rely on repeat or recurring business, such as SaaS (software-as-a-service) subscription-based business models, track other critical metrics:

1. Monthly recurring revenue
2. Annual recurring revenue
3. Average revenue per user
4. Churn: the annual percentage rate at which customers stop subscribing to a service
5. The lifetime value of a customer
6. Customer acquisition cost

## WHY MOST MARKETING ISN'T WORKING

Most smaller companies don't distinguish between sales and marketing. Instead, they merge them into one concept. So most marketing doesn't work because it doesn't exist separate from selling.

A second problem with most companies' marketing is that

owners don't take the time to distinguish themselves from competitors' marketing. As a result, these companies fall into the "commoditization trap"—that is, their product/service is so indistinguishable from the other competitors' that customers default to using price to tell the difference. When you are competing on price, you are now relying more on your salespeople's personalities, presence, and persistence to win over prospective customers.

In the next chapter, I'm going to show you how to develop your competitive advantage based on what makes a business more valuable.

## ACTION STEPS

1. If you want to grow your business, develop your marketing plan. You'll probably need help with this one, so don't go it alone. Reach out for help. For some useful marketing tools, head over to the Resources section of www.DisruptiveSuccessor.com.
2. Identify your metrics and start measuring them.

# CHAPTER 5

# PRODUCT POSITIONING

## HOW TO SET YOURSELF UP FOR MARKET DOMINATION

*"Positioning is all about how your product or service is perceived in the mind of a prospective customer or client. Positioning is not what you do to a product, but how you can change the name, the price, the packaging, or other elements to secure a worthwhile position in the prospect's mind. The basic goal of positioning is not to create something new and different, but to connect your product or service meaningfully to the mental perceptions that already exist in the mind of prospective customers."*

—AL RIES AND JACK TROUT

I've worked with many family businesspeople who are highly skilled in their fields but not very experienced at business ownership. Some have been in business for ten, twenty, or more years but still have significant gaps in their knowledge, particularly when it comes to marketing.

Meet Jeremy Scarlett, a next-generation leader of a fourth-generation family business. When we first met, Jeremy was different from the other design-build landscapers I had coached. He was younger, humbler, hungrier, and more eager to learn. He was a disruptive successor who turned his father's hobby landscape business into one that was dominating in his local market in Ventura, California. When we started working together, my research into an industry association study of landscape company operating costs revealed that landscapers nationwide were spending about 1% of their revenues on advertising and promotion.[13] And typically, these were in places such as yellow pages, internet directories, and vehicle signage. By increasing his marketing spend to almost 5x that of his competitors, Jeremy was able to exploit a gap in the market.

Of course, they had to have better marketing, too. And Jeremy proved that they did by producing a video modeled after a Dollar Shave Club video that went viral on YouTube and carried the brand to a $1B acquisition. Jeremy's video, viewed over 125,000 times, is impressive for any entrepreneur. His 5:1 ratio of spending (really, investing) made Scarlett's Landscaping the first result of most Google searches for landscapers in his region.

And he put supporting systems into place that enabled him to deliver what he promised customers: a better experience hiring a landscaper. He established an in-house team of designers, created a culture that fostered happy employees, invested in software to pump out quality designs with accurate estimates. He also developed a process from designing to constructing that delivered a great experience and invested in software to pump out quality designs with accurate estimates.

During the five years I worked with Jeremy, he grew his small business's revenues from $40,000/month to over $200,000/

month. A disruptive successor with a marketer's mindset, Jeremy crushed area competitors by outspending them on marketing and advertising in a way that got his business noticed. Once he'd earned his spot on page one of Google, he was able to reduce his spending on pay-per-click ads and stay there. These moves made his business more valuable.

## VALUABLE BUSINESSES HAVE THESE IN COMMON

**Valuable businesses must have great products.** Products may be tangible goods or intangible services, ideas, or experiences. The typical decisions that go into developing your products include:

- Design and features.
- Assortment—that is, the range of product lines.
- Branding, packaging, labeling.
- Any additional services that support the sale—for example, after-sales service.
- Any guarantees or warranties, and your return policy.

Questions to answer about your products and why customers buy from you:

- How valuable are your products/services to your customers?
- What value do your products deliver to customers? What needs are they satisfying? Which of your customers' problems are you helping to solve?
- How often do customers buy your product? Do they buy once or in a recurring pattern?
- Are your products made, sold, and delivered in ways that make the company scalable?

**Valuable businesses must also be very differentiated.** Your company may be doing well, so you may think you don't have a positioning problem, but avoid this topic at your peril. If it is not an issue now, it will be soon. If you want to build an industry-dominating company that lasts for generations to come, you need to set your business apart from the competition.

So much of what makes businesses valuable comes down to products and positioning.

The value of your company is based mainly on its differentiation. If you have a better mousetrap, better marketing strategy, or something else unique and valuable to customers, then your company will be worth more, sustain longer, and transfer or sell for a higher price.

Questions to answer about your positioning and why customers buy from you:

- How is the experience of doing business with your company better or different?
- How is your business model better or different—for example, pricing, guarantees, promises?
- Do you assume any leadership in the industry that positions you differently?

*"Within five years, if you're in the same business you are in now, you're going to be out of business."*

*"Your company does not belong in any market where it can't be the best along some valued attribute."*

—PHILIP KOTLER, FATHER OF MODERN MARKETING

**Valuable businesses must also have a supporting business model** that reinforces their positioning. So much of your growth potential has to do with your supporting business model.

Let's say you have established a promise to your customers that you must stand behind. For example, Domino's Pizza promises to deliver in thirty minutes or less. Geico promises that "fifteen minutes could save you 15% or more on car insurance." For Domino's and Geico to keep their promises, they had to establish business processes that supported them. Domino's built low-cost, plain-vanilla stores near college campuses because their primary target market was hungry college students. Geico cut out the frustrating process of getting an insurance quote from an agent by building an easy-to-use online application that compared their quote to competitors'.

Questions to answer about your supporting business model include:

- Have you strategically aligned your business processes to support your marketing message and strategic position?
- Have you established procedures to ensure that you consistently deliver what you promise to customers?
- Has the company established a reputation for delivering its products differently from the competition?
- Have you empowered experts who are capable of delivering the product/service?

**Valuable businesses are built to scale up.** They don't depend on the owner to do the selling, to make and deliver the product/service, or to be the primary person who interfaces with customers. In other words, they are developed with an understanding of the owner's trap.

To be valuable, a product-based business must offer services to support their products: the better the service, the more valuable the company. Similarly, to make service businesses more valuable, they must consider selling their services as products.

## WHAT BUSINESS ARE YOU IN?

You maybe think about your business in terms of its products or services. But maybe not if you have a bigger mindset. For instance, most construction business owners, when asked, "What do you do for work?" or "What business are you in?" might answer, "I am a contractor" or "I own a construction company." Similarly, if you are a plumber, roofer, restaurateur, or software company owner, you might answer, "I own a [insert business here]." But if you are an entrepreneur with a sales and marketing mindset or a business owner with a culture-building, leadership mindset, you are different. You might answer the question by **positioning yourself differently** from your competitors. And your answer might interest customers in further conversation about your business, your position, your purpose, and more. Once you have established a unique position in their minds, your value in their eyes will increase.

### POSITIONING REQUIRES COMPETITIVE ANALYSIS

Any review of your marketing would be incomplete without looking at your competitors. How does your company compare to the top competitors in your market?

Sometimes only one or two differentiated activities are enough to tip the scales in your favor. But if you want to build a moat around your business and increase your value, you will want to have several differentiators. One differentiator can win a tiebreaker. A few differentiators can lead to an industry-dominating position.

It's important to analyze the areas where you can distinguish your offerings from those of your primary competitors. Competitive analysis and positioning is such a broad subject that we'll leave it for other books on marketing.

## POSITIONING AND YOUR COMPANY'S FUTURE

Positioning is about analyzing and planning your company's market penetration strategy. As you contemplate future growth for your business, you will naturally consider expansion into new markets or extension/innovation of your products. Below is a diagram of the Ansoff matrix, which gives you four strategic directions for your company's growth potential. Risk in your venture goes up when you attempt to enter into one or more new markets with one or more new product(s). Investments in new markets with new products (a diversification strategy) have the most considerable risk, whereas entering new markets with an existing product or entering your current market with a new product has only medium risk. Selling more of your current products/services into your existing market is the lowest risk, which is why positioning your business differently in your primary market is the most sensible approach.

## STEPS TO DEVELOPING YOUR COMPETITIVE ADVANTAGE

To develop your competitive advantage, I recommend you identify one or more current strengths of your company that set you apart from competitors. Determining this strength, which often lies in your hidden potential, can help you grow the business. Using a growth discovery process to identify your customer segment's needs and desires compared to those of competitors' segments can reveal your positioning. By mapping out the perceived needs of your target customer, you are looking for unmet demand, or for the tiebreaker that will win you their business.

## ACTION STEP

1. Get close to your customers. Ask your best customers for some feedback about your company to learn your differentiators from their perspective. Ask them, "How are we doing? How do you perceive us versus the competition?"

## CHAPTER 6

# PEOPLE

### THE RIGHT PEOPLE IN THE RIGHT SEATS DOING THE RIGHT THINGS RIGHT

*"Not finance. Not strategy. Not technology. It is teamwork that remains the ultimate competitive advantage, both because it is so powerful and so rare."*

—PATRICK LENCIONI, AUTHOR OF BUSINESS FABLES

Your people are the most valuable asset, so building a great team is critical to building a great company. A team creates the leverage needed to make significant feats possible. And of course, if you want to build a company that can scale or work in your absence, you'll need to build the team first.

And here is where family businesses get tripped up. Because family takes priority, it's not uncommon to see the right person in the wrong seat (i.e., someone who fits into the company culture but not their current role), the wrong person in a seat just because they are a family member, and in some seats nobody at all.

When I work with a disruptive successor, they are typically already the CEO/president or are transitioning into that role. It's critical that this person be the right person for their position. So working with them to make sure they are doing their job right becomes priority number one.

Next, I make sure the team is composed of the right people, in the right seats, doing the right activities.

We can expand this mantra into "Right people, right seats, right activities...Doing things right." This small but smart nuance matters because it focuses on effectiveness (right activities) and efficiency (doing things right).

The right employees are so valuable to a company. You'd think they'd be listed on your balance sheet. Your employees walk out the door every night, and your job is to get them to come back the next day as excited as the day before. But they may leave at any time for any reason, including if they don't like the way you treat them.

For a family business, people are still the most valuable asset, but the dynamic is different because in a family, you come back no matter what. You may have a massive fight with your sibling or parent, but your responsibility to go back to work and give it your all doesn't go away. Sometimes that means a dysfunctional business relationship goes on for too long. Just watch a few episodes of *The Profit*, where Marcus Lemonis fixes failing businesses. Most of these are family businesses, and the problems tend to boil down to the primary driver of the company not listening to or collaborating with the other family members.

Since you and your family members cannot get all the work done, you need to attract and surround yourself with the best talent available. You'll need to hire the best, train them exceptionally well, help them achieve career/personal growth, and reward them well with a paycheck, benefits, and all the other perks that keep employees loyal and performing at their best.

Let's start, though, with the family. Too often, we put our family members in roles they cannot handle. Some see that it's okay to be an underperformer or to be untrained and do your job "good enough" because that is the example the owners set.

Unfortunately, I have seen this too many times in my clients' companies. Maybe someone learns QuickBooks quickly, and they become the go-to person for daily finances. Let's assume it's the founder's wife, as I've seen so many times, and she reliably protects the family's cash and keeps the house bills paid, and everyone else is happy not to have to deal with that stuff themselves. She becomes masterful at minimizing their salaries and income taxes or pushing personal expenses through the business, and there are no complaints until an issue occurs. Maybe they start losing jobs on price, or a consultant comes along and shows how their margins are below industry averages, or they start to bid on larger jobs and cannot win or manage them profitably because they have no job costing systems in place.

Sadly, this has happened because the right person was in the wrong position. The QuickBooks volunteer seemed like a logical choice because of her trustworthiness and fit with the company's core values. But just because she jumped in to solve a problem doesn't mean she was the best suited for the position. Yes, the business saved money by not paying a professional bookkeeper, which resulted in more take-home pay for the owners. But as the company grew, her lack of formal training in accounting and bookkeeping caused weaknesses in their books. Expenses weren't classified consistently or correctly. Their chart of accounts became bloated and messy. And they were unable to tell what their actual job costs were, which made pricing for a predictable profit nearly impossible.

## WHERE DO YOU FIT IN THE BUSINESS?

Let's say you're the son in a family construction business, and you follow Dad around to learn the ins and outs of the company. Perhaps you see this as a passing opportunity to make a few extra dollars and get some work experience. Or perhaps you are as committed to making this a better business as your parents are.

The world is a tough place, as you've come to learn, so joining the family business means that you and your family will stick together like glue. After all, blood is thicker than water, and it's starting to seem that joining this business could be a golden opportunity.

If we look at the company and treat it like any other business, then we are trying to find where skills and competencies meet. Families often spend way too little time examining a family member's fit for a position. Perhaps the business would be better off if they hired someone else. If there is no right opportunity for a family member in the business, then counsel them to help them get a position in another company, industry, or field. Maybe they can come back when you have an opening that fits their competencies and skills.

Typically, you don't need to conduct a core values test with a family member because they probably have the same values as you but not always. I've heard of situations where the young family member is a millennial and does not have similar values to their parents, which can be a problem when the parents are trying to hold them accountable.

I would recommend developing a position description to identify critical accountabilities, competencies, and position outcomes so that when a family member assumes a role, they are held to an established standard. Determine if they can do the job, want to do the job, and understand what is required to do it well.

At the end of a reasonable trial period, typically ninety days, I would sit down with the family and review how well it's working. Would you enthusiastically hire this family member for the position they are in? If the answer is no, then the family must be realistic and think about where to put them.

To scale up your family business, or any business for that matter, you must have the best people. I'll repeat what I learned in business school: A management team of A-players with a C business concept will outperform and out-execute a management team of C-players with a grade A business concept. In other words, people trump the business model, the strategy, and the plan. Every venture capitalist who walked into our classroom said the same thing.

## WHEN TO HIRE

You should hire a new employee when a leader is doing tasks that are beneath their hourly rate of pay.

Recognize when a new person's addition will add value and free up time to drive more sales, revenues, efficiency, and profits into the business.

### THE BIGGEST HIRING MISTAKES

The biggest mistakes I see in hiring are different but related: hiring too fast and keeping a person too long.

1. **Hiring too fast.** You should be quick about hiring. But don't *rush*.
2. **Waiting too long to decide you need a new hire.** You should never hang on to an employee who is underperforming for too long, violates company values, or doesn't

fit in. It's a big mistake costing you future opportunities and causing you present pain.

Too often, smaller businesses and family businesses with strong family values hang on to someone who's not working well too long, because they're worried they won't find a replacement. If you have someone like that at your company, the longer you hold on to them, the more your dissatisfaction will grow, and the more other employees will see that you tolerate unacceptable behaviors, results, or performance. I know you will be relieved when this person leaves and surprised when you find an excellent replacement for them.

I have had many a smaller company hang on to someone they should have replaced a while ago. Every time they finally let that person go and work with me to find a suitable replacement, they remark afterward, "I can't believe I waited so long to do that!"

Hiring with the right timing is only part of the battle. You have to make the right hire, too!

It's so important to spend time hiring the right person because the costs of a bad hire are high in terms of time, money, and motivation.

According to the US Department of Labor, the cost of a bad hire is at least 30% of the employee's first-year earnings. And according to notable hiring experts and creators of Topgrading (an assessment methodology that uses unusually thorough best practices), Geoff and Brad Smart, the price of a bad hire can be as much as 15x the employee's annual salary. But by doing the necessary work up front, you can improve the odds you hire the right person from 14% to 75%. That's a significant increase, and it's worth the effort because the cost of hiring the wrong person is enormous.

Attracting, recruiting, selecting, hiring, onboarding, motivating, challenging, and retaining are all part of the process of building a great team. Let's do a deeper dive into each step and go over some of my recommended best practices.

## WHERE DO YOU FIND THIS A-TEAM PLAYER?

My advice to many of my clients is to ask others in their company, mainly the A- and A-potential players, if they can recommend a friend or past coworker. These people often make the best hiring choices and fit in quickly to the company culture. Internally referred people are 4x better than other hires, according to Geoff Smart.

Next, look within your industry. Make a list of ten people who might know people you should hire. People who wish to relocate to your region can make good hires. People involved in your industry associations can quickly assimilate because they know the industry. But be careful about hiring competitors' employees both because they could be competitors' rejects and because they could hurt your relationship with these competitors.

Advertising for people can take many forms. What I like about common advertising platforms such as ZipRecruiter, Indeed, or LinkedIn is that they offer transparency that has been lacking in the past by allowing candidates and employers to review each other's backgrounds. They also provide some useful scoring and screening tools. The last time I used Indeed, I was able to ask candidates to record responses to some standard qualifying, which gave me a chance to hear each candidate's voice, cadence, and clarity of thinking. This eliminated the need to set up a separate answering machine to screen calls from prospective candidates.

Executive recruiters are another source. Sometimes they are necessary if you need a high level of discretion.

The best way to recruit people to work for your company is to be a destination employer—that is, to be a business people want to come work for. One of my clients, a growing residential and commercial landscape company, is in an industry where it is difficult to find good, qualified employees. We've been working together to build a cohesive culture at his company. The results have been just short of miraculous!

One year ago, we were struggling to find candidates. In the past ninety days, we attracted over 325 résumés for only a few open positions. What's better is that two crews and two leaders at another local residential installation contractor jumped ship to join my client's company. Why? Because my client is doing things better. They've developed a team-first and learning-oriented culture that makes for a motivating and engaging work environment. It's no wonder that employees are finding out about my client and joining them.

As part of building this culture, my client does a great job in public relations and community marketing. Not only do they get free publicity for doing a community landscape project every month, but their trucks are the cleanest fleet in the area, so they easily get noticed. Word has spread, and they have become an attractive employer to join. Offer your employees a bounty for bringing in quality people. It pays you back in spades.

## RECRUITING

Finding talented people is always a challenge. Today, most recruitment is done online through websites such as ZipRecruiter, Indeed, Craigslist, and LinkedIn, but this is continuously changing.

My favorite technique for finding a middle-level management-type person is to take an active marketing approach. Instead of waiting for inbound applications, look on job sites for candidates who have posted their résumés and are in the market for a new job. This is the method executive recruiters use and can often be successful. It may require some ingenuity, determination, and perseverance to fill some positions. But never, ever give up.

## SELECTING

Once you've chosen some good candidates to interview, you need to make sure they fit in with your company and can do the tasks required. I recommend conducting a core values test.

First, you need to develop your core values. To do that, think about those people in your company who embody its best attributes. Define those attributes. Label them. Distill them down to a manageable number; typically, five to seven is enough. If your company is a startup company or has a young culture, have the leaders identify those attributes that have worked in their prior companies. The values you have in one company will often carry over to another.

Once you have identified your core values, you need to put them in place. The process of developing and identifying them can take an hour or more in a workshop setting, but it can take a year or more to cement them into the company culture. It's not enough to wing it or use your gut instinct here.

After that, you need to design some creative questions to ask to determine whether your candidates fit well with them. Suppose you have a core value of teamwork. You'll need to come up with an original question or two to figure out if a candidate is a team player.

You might ask a direct question such as, "What do you enjoy more: working on a team or working alone?" or an oblique one such as, "What is your favorite sport and why?" You might ask them about the teams they played on in high school or college or the ones they worked on in previous jobs. Say things such as, "Describe the dynamics of that team. Did you choose them or not? Who did? How well did they work together as a unit? How would you describe your role on the team?" If they cannot come up with an answer, give them some hints: "For example, were you the leader, influencer, supporter, detail person?" Look for signs that form a pattern. When they are answering questions about their accomplishments, do they use "I" or "we"? This alone may tell you if they are a team player or not.

The key is that if you develop a few questions for each core value, you'll be able to evaluate and grade candidates against each value. If their scores are high enough, then you'll know they're a good culture fit. Do this for each core value. I've seen companies hire the wrong person and then fire them because they missed one essential core value such as teamwork. This mistake can force you to fire someone who is fulfilling a function well but doesn't play well with others.

Next, you need to interview candidates and evaluate whether they have the competencies to complete the objective outcomes (production requirements) of the position. For instance, if you are hiring an account manager to manage $1M in accounts each year, you'll need to know what each candidate's prior experience doing this has been and grade them on it from A to F.

## HIRING THE RIGHT PERSON, STEP BY STEP

Researchers have analyzed the options for evaluating job candidates by effectiveness, and they're worth noting before you wade in:

1. **The Interview Process:** This includes reviewing the résumé, followed by the interview. This process alone gives you only a 14% chance of hiring the right person.
2. **Reference Checking:** Following up on references increases your hiring hit rate to a 26% chance.
3. **Personality Testing:** By adding personality testing, you increase your chances to 38 percent.
4. **Abilities Testing:** Job-related skills and abilities tests increase your chances to 54 percent.
5. **Interest Testing:** Assessing an individual's interests to see if they relate to the position increases your odds to 66% because these are an individual's natural motivators to do the job.
6. **Job Match:** Assess candidates using a reliable job match assessment to increase your chances to a staggering 75 percent.[14]

I am currently wrapping up some one-on-one coaching with a client who was focused on finding a VP of operations for a company with fifteen employees doing $2.5M per year. To find our perfect person, we employed an approach I adapted from Geoff and Brad Smart's "hiring toolbox" from their Topgrading® program.

The first step is to define the position, getting clear on the competencies, attributes, and expected outcomes specific to the job. We clarify the core values that we'll use to evaluate candidates. We then develop questions to grade each person against each competency and outcome.

We want them to answer questions about past employment and education so we can form a complete history of each candidate. Making it very clear, in advance, that you are going to contact references will increase the likelihood that they'll speak honestly about their role, responsibilities, and results.

I recommend 3 × 3 × 3 interviewing—talking with three different people for three hours at three different times and places each. You can get a better read on a person with that many touches. After three hours of interviewing, a person cannot lie or hold up a facade. They become more authentic over time as the stress and pressure build up. If you have three different people interviewing them, you can get three different opinions on them. And by interviewing someone at three different times and places, you see how they behave in different settings.

After meeting with one of his VP of operations candidates, my client remarked that he felt this person did too much talking. He was concerned that the candidate might not be a good listener. I suggested they meet outside the office over lunch or coffee and see if he observed the same thing. Was he just nervous, or was talking too much his usual style? Another touch made sense. After all, he would have to see the candidate for forty hours a week if he hired him.

Another technique that can work well is to try someone out for a day or a week with pay to see how they fit. It is always worthwhile but not always practical. I once was interviewed this way. One of the most successful business incubators in California hired me as a consultant for a week to see if the fit between us was right. It wasn't a good fit, so it seemed at the time, but the woman in the next office over might have been vying for my position. She would shortly after that become the COO and founder's partner in marriage!

You've now completed a series of lengthy interviews in tandem with another person on the team—one person to take notes, the other person to be the interviewer. The candidates have been graded on their competency. They've been evaluated for culture fit using questions about your core values and purpose. You've done a reference check to confirm what they have told you is correct.

Next, you might ask them to complete a behavioral assessment to learn more about their preferences, workplace motivators, behavioral patterns, and emotional intelligence. An assessment like this will be useful in coaching them and integrating them into the team by helping you understand how they communicate.

I also recommend you bring in a seasoned advisor or another key employee as a third party for an objective perspective. We are trained to look from A to Z at your hiring and selection process for gaps.

## ONBOARDING

After the hiring decision is made based on productivity fit, culture fit, and competencies/skills fit, you need to make sure the new hire is adequately onboarded into your company culture so they can fit in as quickly as possible.

This means they must know the company's purpose or mission statement. They must know and be able to recall the core values. They must be aware of the company's vision and plan for continued success and what their role in that success is going to look like. They should have a job description with accountability metrics for their position. And they should receive any required or recommended training for their job.

But it should not end here. I have all my clients take a behavioral assessment—for example, DISC or Kolbe. And then we share the results with their colleagues. It contributes to the health of the team if the new employees know the results of their teammates' assessments.

## MOTIVATING AND RETAINING

I like to make sure people are engaged and challenged in their jobs and that they are learning all the time. This matters more than anything. It even trumps how much money they are making because people's top priority is to be in a position that is fulfilling. Fair pay is just an end product of the work they do. I want to make sure they are receiving coaching either from their superiors or from an outside professional who is keen on developing the capacity and capabilities of my client.

I make sure we make work fun by identifying a critical measure and making a game out of it. For example, one of my clients was having an issue with people showing up late to work, so they gave out poker chips to people who showed up early or on time. At the end of the month, they could redeem their poker chips toward useful items such as water bottles or coupons at popular establishments. I also always make sure to incorporate some activities that create fun outside of the work environment. It could be a company barbecue, a trip to a go-karting track, a company volleyball game, or a pro sports event. It doesn't matter if it's not the ultimate event because there will always be another one in a few months.

## COMPENSATION IN A FAMILY BUSINESS

Compensation is another big subject that can be thorny in family businesses. I recommend you develop structured compensation ranges for each position. And when it comes to compensating family members, they are paid no more than a modest 5- 10% premium over the programmed amount.

Whenever possible, you'll want to think about how to have a balanced incentive compensation plan so that performance incentives—for example, commissions, bonuses, and so on—are balanced with wages, base salary, perks, and so on.

In developing your compensation program, lavish salaries provide ease in hiring talent but carry high fixed costs and a considerable company cost with no promise of performance. Too much focus on incentives is too risky for most employees. During miserable performance years, high salaries can be a heavy burden for your company. Significant incentives offer a way of self-funding compensation based on performance, but when performance objectives are not hit and monies not paid out, this can result in a significant turnover. So think carefully through this conundrum. What is fair and best for all parties? What behaviors are you trying to incentivize?

## THE VALUE OF ENGAGED EMPLOYEES

Since Gallup began tracking employee engagement in 2000, they found that, on average, 17.2% of an organization's workforce is actively disengaged. Gallup describes an actively disengaged worker as someone who is "unhappy and unproductive at work and liable to spread negativity to coworkers." In other words, they are people who don't like their jobs and aren't afraid to let others know it. Gallup also found that an actively disengaged employee costs their organization $3,400 for every $10,000 of salary—34%. In a company of 100 employees, with a median salary of $60,000/year, that means disengaged employees cost the company $346,800 each year.[15] [16]

So it's worth it to invest in the things you can do to increase employee engagement. First, you can work on building a durable culture so that your company becomes one where people want to work. Second, you can conduct regular one-on-one coaching meetings with each of your direct reports. If you don't have a transparent chain of command in your organization, you can hold one-on-one coaching meetings using a peer group or collaborative partner model.

The point here is that monthly check-ins with people are very helpful in motivating them to perform better. You are helping teammates see where they are stuck, coaching them through those spots, and providing feedback on areas that matter to them. I have several forms for these one-on-ones that will help with structuring these conversations around your teammates' performance, goals, challenges, and direct reports.

These regular one-on-one meetings need to be quarterly at a minimum, monthly on average, and weekly if there is rapid change happening in your organization, and they should be part of your quarterly and annual performance review process. Why wait twelve months to give someone feedback on how they are doing? Regular performance reviews make the process much more informal. They allow you to build trust and foster open communication with your people.

## A NOTE ABOUT VIRTUAL TEAMS

These days, so many companies I coach have virtual teams. One client I worked with had employees in San Diego, Tampa, Philadelphia, Israel, and throughout Eastern Europe. (If I were to assemble my team of outsourced service providers, I would have to organize people from Atlanta, San Diego, Florida, India, and the United Kingdom. It's crazy how distributed our workforce can be.)

When your team is not co-located, you have to create hangout spaces for them to build the kind of camaraderie you typically find at the water cooler. You must go to extra lengths to make sure people are connecting and conversing. Fortunately, there are technological solutions. Popular tools my clients and team have used include Slack, Basecamp, Google Hangouts, Zoom, Skype, Team Viewer, and Microsoft Teams. New tools are created all the time to address the need for togetherness.

To build the dynamics of teams, I have them perform some intimate and challenging exercises with each other. One is to compare people's behavioral preferences and styles using DISC. Another trust-building activity, which is highly effective but also more confronting, is a team effectiveness exercise that I credit to Pat Lencioni, author of *The Five Dysfunctions of a Team*. The behaviors of each team member are shared with the team and categorized as helpful/effective and harmful/ineffective. The group does this in a positive tone so that people feel they are getting constructive feedback, not being criticized. I have seen many teams come together better after this activity because it encourages members to bring their best selves to the team.

## REVIEWS VERSUS COACHING

You'll notice that I haven't talked about performance reviews, probably because nobody likes to give them or receive them. But if you view them as opportunities to coach your direct reports, they can be very compelling and impactful. Ideal team players (i.e., humble, hungry, and smart) will welcome performance reviews as opportunities to learn and grow.

I have some review processes I recommend to my clients, and I would offer one to you here, but I find that review processes change frequently and that most companies already have one that can be modified and improved.

## EVALUATING YOUR TEAM

Trust is foundational to building a strong team. In both family and nonfamily businesses, an absence of trust and a fear of conflict are common problems. In family businesses, conflict is most likely due to family members' personal histories and established biases. For companies where team members aren't familiar with each other, I recommend starting by having everyone share their personal history and life experiences in order to deepen members' connection to each other and the team.

To build a cohesive and functional team, it is ideal to start with team players who exhibit healthy behaviors. Healthy behaviors are those that align with your core values. Someone who does not exhibit these behaviors does not belong on your team.

The folks at GE taught us that we should rate our teammates based on how productive they are and how well they fit in with the company culture and values. Using a simple matrix (shown below), we can rate people on the x-axis based on their productivity and the y-axis based on how well they fit in with culture and core values.

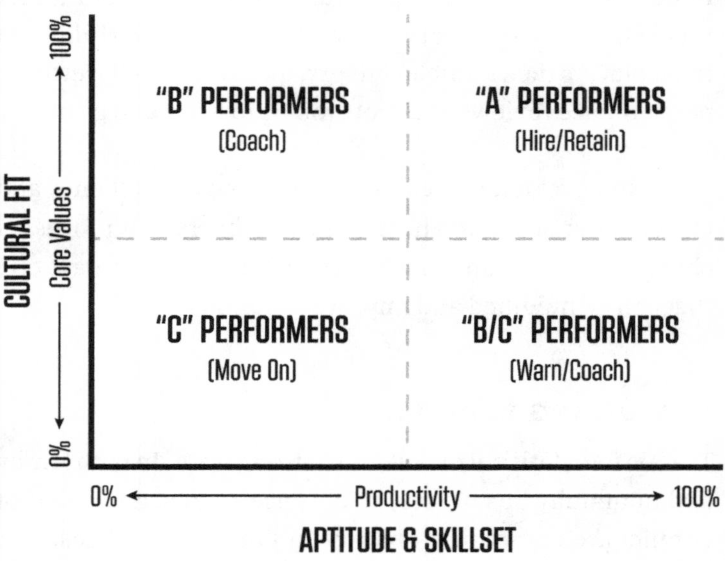


Using this kind of a matrix, we focus our time, attention, and compensation on the A-players because they produce the most significant results. We remove the C-players, possibly helping them with outplacement but not spending too much time with them because they drag down the performance and productivity of the team. Spending too much time with C-players is what we call the C-player trap, which we want to avoid at all costs. Then we have our B-players. If they share our values and culture, then we coach them on how to be more productive. If they are highly productive but don't share our values and culture, we can tolerate them for only so long before we must move them out of the company.

For obvious reasons, moving family out of the company isn't as easy as moving out nonfamily members. But in the end, you must look at your family business as a business first and do what is best for the company. If a family member doesn't fit, you must do the unthinkable and fire them. You can do this in a very civilized, humane, and caring fashion so that the family member lands in a better place.

## FIRING FAMILY MEMBERS

There may come a time when you must fire a family member. It is among the most difficult things you will ever do in a family business, yet it may be for the good of the family, the company, and the individual being fired.

Here's a scenario to consider:

Suppose you have a family member who doesn't play by the same rules as the others, rules you have created. What do you do?

You have to draw a hard line here and do what you would do with any other such employee. It may take some time to address this situation, but it's cancerous and toxic. You must fire this family member. Perhaps you need to do it with care and grace so as not to affect your relationship. After all, you still need to see and relate to this family member, and that's not going to change. But you have to do the right thing for your company and its culture. Otherwise, you are setting a bad example, and others will expect this double standard to apply to them, too.

Generally, when thinking about people who don't fit in the company, you have to choose:

- Train/Coach?
- Dump/Replace?
- Reposition/Realign?

## ACTION STEPS

1. Do you have the best people your money can buy? Are your people and processes driving industry-leading profitability? If not, make a list of those people who are not performing at the level you believe they should. If they don't fit the culture, you may need to fire them. If they fit the culture but not the position, try to relocate them. If they are in the right job but lack the training to elevate them in the organization, then give them the proper training. For help with these distinctions, download our People Evaluator Tool from www.DisruptiveSuccessor.com.
2. Download more tools to help you coach your people and live your core values:
   A. One-on-One Coaching of Managers and start regular coaching of your people
   B. Define your Core Values exercise

# CHAPTER 7

# PEOPLE

## DEVELOPING LEADERS

*"Before you are a leader, success is all about growing yourself. When you become a leader, success is all about growing others."*

—JACK WELCH

Imagine the size of your family business in a few years. How many total employees do you have? How many millions of dollars in sales is your company doing? Now look around at your current leaders in the company. How many of them have the skills to take you to that level of sales? Have they done it before? Do they have the tools they need?

Do you have other family members who will be taking over management roles? Do they have what it takes to do the job?

What about employees who have been with the company for decades and were probably hired by the founder. Are they still a fit for the business under a next-generation leader's management?

Chances are, you need a new generation of leaders and managers to take your business to the next level. You'll probably have to say goodbye to some of the older people who were your go-to staff members because they won't cut it at this next level. Before we talk about the other leaders in the company and how to develop them, let's first discuss the current leadership.

How do you know if your parent's leadership has what is needed to take the company to the next level?

Look at the results.

- Is your company experiencing year-over-year sales growth?
- Is your parent developing a next generation of leaders in your family business?
- Is training, learning, and mentorship part of the fabric of your business?
- Do you have a written business plan with clearly stated goals against which you measure success?

If you see leadership that is exacting, exciting, and forward-thinking, then you have a leader with a vision and a plan. If not, then the current leadership isn't inspiring change, growth, or a better future. Both situations present a dynamic opportunity.

If your parent is driving the vision of a great business, then learn from him/her. If s/he can inspire you to grow, change, and become a better person and entrepreneur, then stand with him/her as a business leader.

But if you are a disruptive successor, what got you here isn't going to get you there. You'll need to show your parent that you have the vision to grow the business so that they trust you to take the lead. You'll need to demonstrate your effectiveness as a growing young leader. You'll need to sell your parent on your vision for the company. And, of course, you'll need to "show them the money." If you want to get your parent to invest in your vision, show them how you will make a return on that investment.

Your parent is more than likely trying to figure out whether you are ready to take over the business. They are testing you to see if you are prepared to handle this challenge responsibly. Perhaps they have given you a small allocation of funds to make a purchase, add some new talent, expand to another location, or manage an office, budget, profit and loss statement, or division of the business. Perhaps they have relinquished authority over something that used to be their domain. After all, if they want to build a company that can be transferred (or sold), they will have to train their second-in-command.

There are some telltale signs of this transition in the process. Have they asked you what you would do if you were running the company? Have they taken time away from the business—one week, two weeks, or a month—and given you "acting CEO" privileges during that time to see how well you do? Have they invested in your learning at seminars, workshops, and the like?

If you are going to be the next-generation leader of your family business, you will need to demonstrate wise, intelligent, and ethical decision making before your parents hand over the keys to the kingdom they built.

Be honest with yourself. If you are not confident that you are ready to lead the family business, you have work to do. You may need to hire an executive/business coach, seek out industry and business mentors, join a peer group that supports your emergence as a leader and manager, and identify your strengths and weaknesses with the help of your coach, mentors, employees, and peers. Participate in personal development programs. Develop your abilities as a leader. Read more business books, take more courses, and learn, learn, learn.

## ATTRIBUTES OF GREAT LEADERS

Building your company is going to require great leaders who can create followership. What are the attributes of great leaders? They listen to others with empathy. They are learners with long-term perspectives. The long-term outlook is so important because business is not a game that you win or lose in a finite amount of time; business is an infinite game that you play as long as the company exists.

### BEHAVIORAL CHARACTERISTICS OF GREAT LEADERS

Leaders who exhibit high emotional intelligence (EQ) will find it easier to get others to follow them. In his book Emotional Intelligence, Daniel Goleman discusses things such as social and emotional regulation and intrapersonal/interpersonal regulation (understanding of self and others). When assessing new potential hires, look at how they score on the EQ assessment. A high score likely translates to the ability to create followership.[17]

EQ has two components in the context of leadership:

The first is EQ—Self: what goes on inside of you.

Self-awareness is the ability to recognize and understand your moods, emotions, and drives, as well as your effect on others. Self-regulation is the ability to control or redirect disruptive impulses and feelings: the propensity to suspend judgment and think before acting.

EQ—Others: what goes on between you and others.

Social awareness is the ability to understand the emotional makeup of other people and how your words and actions affect them. Social regulation is your ability to influence the emotional clarity of others by managing relationships and building networks.

## COMPETENCY CHARACTERISTICS OF GREAT LEADERS

Leaders need to be bold, visionary, and decisive in order to create followership. Leaders also need to be developers of other leaders, not micromanagers, to bring out the best in others.

Leaders are learners who have the tools to work through the challenges that come with leadership, such as building a team, communicating, making difficult strategic choices, funding projects, making investments, or raising capital to support continued growth.

Typically, before making any key hires, I have my clients create a list of desired competencies to evaluate each candidate against. Not doing this leaves a significant step out of the hiring process and leads to more bad hires.

## KEY RESPONSIBILITIES OF GREAT LEADERS

The responsibilities of leaders are many and varied. They differ from management responsibilities because leaders are involved in:

- Creating and selling the vision
- Setting direction and priorities
- Providing resources, tools, and support to meet goals
- Focusing their team on their vital few priorities and not their many trivial to-dos
- Defining and structuring the organizational culture
- Helping to develop the systems
- Modeling good work habits
- Spending time with high-profile customers to maintain a customer-focused business
- Spending time with key employees to maintain an employee-focused business
- Driving results
- Developing people
- Improving continuously

As a senior leader and an owner of the business, you are responsible for encouraging your people to learn by reading books, taking video courses, taking workshops, participating in a peer group, and receiving coaching and mentoring.

### JUSTIN'S STORY

You'll remember Justin, who took over K&D Landscaping from his parents and grew revenues 10x in four years. He didn't do all his learning alone. He surrounded himself with talented, committed people who shared his thirst for excellence and knowledge. He developed himself as a leader and then established leaders on his team.

Justin has demonstrated excellent decision making. His wisdom as a leader has grown since we started working together. He's always learning more about leadership, management, and business, and increasing his legal, financial, and industry knowledge to stay on top of his game.

When Justin took over the business, he took a fresh approach to the company. He knew it needed an overhaul of systems and processes and that the books and financial records needed cleaning up. He knew he needed new people to realize the vision of the business that was forming in his mind.

He knew that he needed to begin with the end in mind. Where was he trying to take this business? What was his vision? Would the company transfer hands again, or would they sell it? (By building exit options early, as all entrepreneurs should, you can ensure that your business is buyer and seller ready, which will help it sell for a premium.)

All we were talking about at this point was having a vision for future possibilities. Justin and his family may ultimately transfer or hand down the business, but either way, he needs to think big and bet smart. That is, assuming you've gotten past the parent-child rivalry issues.

If you have, then your parent should be getting out of the way to let you run the business and demonstrate your command of the company. They have undoubtedly taught you everything they know. Now they need to get out of the way. If you are as successful as they were, you can provide them with a residual income for as long as the business is in the family, which could be the rest of your life. If you can grow the profits of the firm, they will enjoy a premium benefit, and the business can be transferred for an attractive, negotiated purchase price. In other words, you can make yourself and your parents wealthy.

An investment in a small business can have a much higher return than an investment in many other asset classes. An investment in your business, as I will show you in a later chapter, can have a return on investment of 20–50% per year. When you compare this to any other investment vehicle—stocks, bonds, mutual funds, and the like—you can see that's a tidy sum.

To accomplish this, you will need to learn about finance, legal, taxes, strategy, leadership, management, and so much more. It will be the best education and the ride of your life!

## ACTION STEPS

1. Request your free sample EQ Assessment: email me at Jon@TheGoldhillGroup.com with the subject line, "I read your book and want a sample EQ Assessment."

# CHAPTER 8

# PEOPLE

## WHAT YOU NEED TO KNOW ABOUT CONFLICT AND NEGATIVE COMMUNICATION STYLES

*"Wherever you see a successful business, someone once made a courageous decision."*

—PETER F. DRUCKER, AUTHOR, FATHER OF MODERN MANAGEMENT

Any family dynamic can be complicated. Even when things are not contentious on the surface, there may be underlying issues, feelings, or negative emotions that can prevent the company from reaching its full potential. As a leader, you will have to be mindful of psychological and behavioral problems that don't belong in the workplace. For instance, sibling rivalry, father-son, and mother-daughter rivalry are all common.

Let's take, for example, the case of Markson Contracting, a first-generation family-run construction company operating in Costa Mesa, California. (This is a hypothetical company I created for illustration purposes, based on my experience with a wide array of companies.) The founder and patriarch, Joe Markson, is in his seventies. A self-made man, he built his company from scratch and became very successful. But hard work over many decades has taken a toll on his body.

Joe knows that it's soon going to be time to hand over the reins to his three sons, Eric, Adam, and John. Because his sons have worked in the business all their lives, Joe has left it up to them to run the day-to-day and spends most of his time focusing on his health.

At the age of fifty-three, Eric is the eldest and would seem like the logical choice to run the company. However, Eric is resentful and distrustful of his younger siblings. He spends much time trying to "be the boss" and hold sway over operations, often directing unfounded criticism at his brothers.

Although they joined the family business later in life, John and Adam are hard workers. John has a degree in IT engineering and is mostly responsible for choosing and implementing software to help the company compete with other contractors in the area. Unfortunately, Eric has an inherent distrust of technology and continually challenges the solutions John brings to the table.

Adam functions as a job-site project manager. Although Adam does a good job and is well-liked by customers, Eric often undermines him, which leads to conflict and delays. As a result, it is difficult to get new business because they are always behind schedule. Often, Eric will dig in his heels just to spite Adam, who then has to suffer the fallout.

Despite the constant conflict, Joe continues to allow Eric to run the day-to-day, hoping that things will eventually settle down.

At this stage, every critical business decision is driven by conflict and personality. There is no mentorship, no clear succession plan, as Joe seems content to let his sons bicker their way through each day. They don't communicate well, and there is no consensus or overarching plan to move them forward.

Where do they go from here?

## RECOGNIZING NEGATIVE COMMUNICATION STYLES

Dr. John Gottman, a pioneering therapist, identifies four negative communication styles that he calls the "Four Horsemen of the Apocalypse," which are disastrous to any relationship. Even though Gottman is best known for marriage counseling, the same principles apply here.

### CRITICISM

Complaints are one thing. Criticism is entirely another. A complaint focuses on a specific issue, whereas criticism attacks a person. When criticized, people feel like they are under attack. When there are close family dynamics in play, this behavior can escalate quickly.

Eric criticizes Adam's decisions on the job site. He also attacks and ridicules John's attempts to digitize their operations. He fails to consider the underlying issues that lead them to the decisions they make and uses criticism to keep them in line. No progress is made in any direction.

### CONTEMPT

Contempt takes criticism to another level. It mocks, ridicules, disrespects, and disregards with words, deeds, or gestures meant to make the recipient feel worthless and inept.

Criticism attacks the person, but contempt attacks their moral character and gives the speaker a superior position.

Eric shows great contempt toward Adam on the job site. If anything goes wrong whatsoever, he calls Adam out and usually in front of the customer. Several times, Eric has made Adam feel so worthless that Adam simply walked off the job. Adam believes there will come a day when he walks away and does not return.

### DEFENSIVENESS

Defensiveness is self-protection in the face of an attack. Usually, it's a counterattack that casts blame on an event, circumstance, or another person. When we are unfairly accused, we tend to look for anything that will make the accuser back off. When we are defensive, nobody is taking responsibility, and the conflict continues to escalate.

John blamed Eric for refusing to learn the software. But Eric, feeling criticized, spoke up loudly and said, "I never agreed with the decision to buy that program!"

### STONEWALLING

Stonewalling is generally a response to contempt. In response to an attack, a person withdraws, does not respond, or shuts down entirely. To them, this might seem like the only way to act. Keep in mind that usually, stonewalling happens when strikes have been sustained over some time. It's a feeling of being completely overwhelmed to the point where rational discussion is not possible. Walking away can make things worse, but sometimes it's the only way to make things stop.

Adam's anger with Eric over his constant attacks on the job site has led to a lot of bad feelings between the brothers. Sadly, it has seeped into his family life as well, and now he has a tough time facing issues with any family member, not just Eric.

Although there is no rational excuse for any of these bad behaviors, we also shouldn't expect that just because the Marksons are family, all should be forgiven. The brothers' feud is not unusual. What's missing here is some oversight by Markson Sr.

Had Joe been more involved in shaping his sons' roles and instilling a sense of shared purpose, they may not have reached the point that they are at right now.

## HEALTHY AND UNHEALTHY CONFLICT

Conflict in business and families can be healthy or unhealthy. It's important to distinguish between the two. Simply put, when conflict is issue-oriented, it is healthy. When conflict becomes personal, it becomes unhealthy.

Unhealthy conflict is usually the result of some preexisting bias or prejudice toward another person. When this happens in a family business, it can cause people to avoid sensitive topics (especially ones such as succession and transition planning), and it can lead to splintered working relationships or even prevent the business from transitioning to the next generation.

Healthy conflict is typically issue-oriented or results-oriented and can relate to disagreements about an approach or a decision made without full commitment from the team. Teams that trust one another engage in passionate dialogue around decisions key to the organization's success. They do not hesitate to disagree with, challenge, and question one another in the spirit of discovering the truth, finding the best answers, and making the right decisions.

Get clear on whether conflict in your business is healthy or unhealthy so you can proceed accordingly. If a battle has become toxic, then it's time to work out your differences, which can be done through a conversation or structured dialogue process using a counselor, coach, facilitator, mediator, or neutral third party.

## GROUND RULES FOR EFFECTIVE CONFLICT ELIMINATION

Over the years, I have come across and modified others' ground rules to model effective teaming. I believe these work well to eliminate conflict from relationships. Here are my ground rules you can use to bring things back into balance between people:

- Keep an open mind to other people's ideas and concepts.
- Eliminate the "I know that" attitude from your listening, as it destroys teaming and can turn conflict personal.
- Say what you mean, mean what you say. Oh, and don't say it mean. Honor all agreements you made, as this communicates trust like no other behavior.
- Do what you say you will do. Not finishing tasks or following through on commitments can result in conflict that can become personal.

- Finish what you start. An organization's integrity depends on individual integrity.
- Stay in communication. Teaming works well when people process and complete commitments that are in alignment with agreements and deliverable dates. Commit to staying in communication about open items.
- Celebrate successes. Build momentum and energy on your team by stopping to recognize achievements, both large and small, and sharing them with the team.
- Maintain open, honest, direct communication. When you stop being fair and transparent, issues can quickly arise, leading to deep conflict.
- Neutralize your perception of other people. Focus on the problem or issue, not the person.
- Shower others with praise. The quickest way to someone's heart just may be through their ego. Validate them for their contributions, and make sure they know you see their value to your company. Send them appreciation emails. Three lines are about all it takes to let someone know you recognize what they do for the company.
- Don't blame, justify, or deny responsibility. Consider the fact that maybe you're causing the problem and take responsibility for what belongs to you. Be the owner and master of your life and business. Remove the "story" (excuses, reasons) from your situation. Take feedback from others. Learn from it instead of fighting it.
- Foster a "win-win" mentality instead of a "me versus them" mentality. Show others you're not greedy when it comes to winning, being in the spotlight, praise, or additional compensation. Show them that you have their back. Ask their opinion on a variety of decisions and topics. Let them shine as well.

## DEALING WITH CONFLICT

By preparing for difficult, high-stakes conversations, you can transform anger and hurt feelings into powerful dialogue and make it safe to talk about almost anything. This can take some serious effort on your part. However, it is worth it, especially when you're dealing with family members and wounds and hurt feelings can be profound.

In any conflict situation, you will need to first go through the internal process of getting clear on your needs. Then you should focus exclusively on the other person's needs. Only then can you express yourself in a neutral and calm tone of voice and expect the other person to hear what you say and receive it well.

In most conflict resolution conversation models, the steps look like this:

1. Identify the issue AND provide a specific example of the behavior or situation you want to see changed.
2. Describe your emotions about the issue and clarify what is at stake. If you identify your contribution to the problem, it shows the other person that not only s/he is to blame and that you take some responsibility.
3. Indicate your desire to resolve the issue.
4. Invite the person to respond. Be open to hearing their side of the issue and their desire for things to be different going forward.

Some situations are more straightforward than others. You can't always seek a resolution. Recently, I worked with a family business where the dynamic between the owner and his stepson was impossible to fix in the time we had. We did some communication exercises and they expressed appreciation for each other's contributions to the business. But it became clear to me that they weren't going to resolve their issues in one session. That would require regular, probably weekly, counseling sessions based on basic communication exercises. I didn't feel that they wanted to do the work because our conversations often quickly got away from the exercise format. Things would improve for a couple of months, maybe longer, and then they would be right back to where they were when I first met them. The time investment it would take to fix their issues, which had existed for decades, was simply too much. Eventually, the son threw his hands up and said, "I'm done. Here is my thirty-day notice."

Other times, the foundation of the relationship is more durable and the issues are worth working through. When I assess whether a problem is fixable, I try to identify if there is the will to fix it. When people have the will to improve things, they take all measures possible to do so.

## DECISIONS, DECISIONS, DECISIONS

You are called to make decisions every day. Do you know which decisions should be made alone and which in the company of others? What about family members? What decisions should you include them in? Some of your choices are difficult ones you may shy away from because they involve conflict. Others are easy. Knowing the difference matters.

The faster you can make decisions, the faster your company will excel. But people won't always agree with your choices. It's essential to understand the different **types** of decisions and **styles** of decision making so that you can choose the most appropriate one for any given circumstances. Without a clear understanding of this, tension can and will erupt.

Your ability to make the right decisions fast will directly impact the growth of your business. But there are some decisions you should take time with, such as those that affect the future of the company—for example, those concerning strategy, large investments, or significant hires. Two common mistakes people make are they make the tough decisions either too slowly or too hastily.

When you delegate decision making to others, you can scale faster. Strategic and financial decisions are like the trunk of a tree. The trunk of the tree is the foundation of the business. Other decisions are like branches, which are further away from the foundation. These can be made by others, independently of the leadership team. The more choices you can delegate further down the chain of command, the more you can focus on the bigger picture. To accomplish this, you must teach and model decision making. Finally, you must guide your employees to know the difference between a branch decision and a trunk decision.

If you don't make decisions, what follows is stagnation and repetition, which leads to lackluster results and people feeling stuck. Of course, people need data and facts to make decisions, but how much data is enough? The answer is, when you have enough to guide you to make a decision that is 80% right or more. You must balance your intuition with your intellect. It helps to know what your biases and blind spots are. Also, you must balance your decision-making style with how you exert your power. If you are commanding in your power style, then perhaps you need to be more collaborative in making decisions.

## TYPES OF DECISIONS

Decisions can be classified as tactical or strategic, programmed or nonprogrammed, basic or routine, planned or off-the-cuff, policy or operational, administrative or executive. You need to consider what type of decision you are making before you decide the style with which you'll make it.

Programmed decisions are typically recurring ones that require objective judgment and relate to organizational, operational, research, or opportunity decisions. Examples might include ordering inventory, granting an employee paid time off, and disciplinary action of a lower-level manager or employee.

Nonprogrammed decisions are often personal, strategic, or crisis related. They are not routine, require very subjective judgment, and are typically reserved for top-level management. Examples might include the purchase of equipment, implementation of a new software or technology tool, and market positioning or branding.

## STYLES OF DECISION MAKING

Styles are probably more familiar to you. Here are some common ones:

- Consensus (where the group decides by shared agreement)
- Democratic or Popular Vote (where the group votes)
- Collaborative (where a decision is reached by negotiated agreement)
- Consultative (where a subset decides)
- Autocratic or Command (where one person decides)

## THE ISSUE, DISCUSS, RECOMMEND MODEL

When the team is involved in decision making, I recommend a simple issue-processing framework that helps you to identify the real issue and dig deep enough to get at the root cause. First, discuss the matter by asking questions and gathering facts. It's crucial that these questions not be asked in a way that leads the person responding to a specific answer. Once everyone has weighed in on the discussion and all clarifying questions have been asked, it's time to solve the issue. You can go around the room round-robin style to get as many viewpoints and recommendations as possible. As people chime in, the solution starts to present itself, either through repetition or when the person who brought up the issue feels they've heard the correct answer or approach.

When someone brings an issue to the table, they might frame it the following way:

1. How do I ___?
2. This issue is important to me because of ___.
3. What I have done to date is ___.
4. What I want the group to help me with is ___.

In this approach, there are eight steps to making the best decision. They are:

1. *Define the decision*: What's the question?
2. *Identify its importance to you.*
3. *Decide:* What are the decision criteria?
4. *Identify the alternatives.*
5. *Evaluate the alternatives*: What are the facts?
6. *Make preliminary choices.*
7. *Assess the risk.*

8. *Make a decision.*

## ACTION STEPS

1. Learn the negative communication styles—and avoid them.
2. Deal with conflict using conflict resolution models.

CHAPTER 9

# PRIORITIES

## MANAGE YOUR TIME AND ENERGY

*"Identify your problems, but give your power and energy to solutions."*

—TONY ROBBINS, SELF-HELP AUTHOR, SPEAKER, LIFE COACH

Let's get back to K&D Landscaping for a moment because this chapter dives into how Justin has been so successful. The route to building a world-class company looks linear in retrospect. But all along the way, he had to create new processes, hire potential performers, fire nonperformers, deal with setbacks from overspending on some large clients, and manage the business remotely through the COVID-19 pandemic.

Justin has chosen to continuously study the best practices of the best companies in his industry. He has and forged relationships with and learned from CEOs in the landscape industry and in other sectors.

But, the secret behind all of this was that Justin learned to manage his time and energy to get maximum power (output) and achieve his priorities. To master this, he has participated in some Tony Robbins workshops on energy management, time management, and mental and emotional state management.

If you are going to lead your family's business to a new level, you'll need to manage your energy and your time to get maximum leverage. You'll need to think in terms of priorities and understand how power, energy, and time are connected to getting the right stuff done.

Here's a quick physics lesson. Power is the rate at which work is done or energy is used. It is equal to the amount of work done divided by the time the work takes. Here's a simple formula that links energy and power:

Energy = Power × Time

Or conversely

Power = Energy ÷ Time

If you divide your energy by your time, you get power. So if you want to magnify your power, you'll want to increase your energy **and** do it in less time. Make sense? From high school math, we learned that in equations like this, the larger the top number (or numerator) and the smaller the bottom number (or denominator), the larger the answer. So doing both—increasing your energy and decreasing the time it takes to do the work—gives you an increase in power. If you want to be more powerful, you'll need to think differently about how you spend your time and how you manage your energy.

## PRIORITY ACCOMPLISHMENT = ENERGY MANAGEMENT ÷ TIME MANAGEMENT

Most experts agree that energy management is more important than time management. To accomplish your goals, identify your priorities and then make the best use of your time and work with peak energy levels. I recommend you work on high-priority, high-impact activities during your peak energy periods. For me, usually that's the first half of the day or after a good exercise session. I can increase the duration and frequency of these peak energy periods by getting good quality sleep and regular exercise, eliminating distractions such as my cellphone, working on stuff that energizes me, and scheduling my highest-priority tasks during peak energy periods.

## BUT FIRST, A WORD ABOUT YOUR MINDSET

It's been my experience that for your business to change, you must change. That means before your company can improve, you need to see the business you want it to become. Then become the change. That means working on your mindset.

It's also been my experience that most small businesses are run by a founder who spends most of their time in their skills zone, which means they lose out on spending their time elsewhere. Now, if the founder has recognized that they have certain unique abilities and knows well enough to surround themselves with others who have compatible unique capabilities, then we're off to the races. But chances are, your parent/founder didn't have the benefit of learning this modern management technique because they were busy starting and running the business. Most people didn't learn all this stuff back then. But now that information flows so freely through books, the internet, podcasts, and wherever else you consume media, working on your mindset is essential.

You will need to engineer your mindset if your business is going to change. Your parent can't teach you because this is new stuff for them, too. Mindset is the modern psychology of success. After decades of research, Carol S. Dweck, a world-renowned psychologist, showed how success in school, sports, work, and almost every area of human endeavor can be dramatically influenced by how we think about our talents and abilities. According to her, people with a fixed mindset are those who believe their abilities are fixed and are less likely to flourish than those with a growth mindset—those who believe that their abilities can be developed.

Just because your parent did something one way doesn't mean you need to do it that way, too. You will need to manage your time differently. After all, your parent probably got many things done, but they might have ignored the sort of high-level types of activities addressed in this book. They might have hyperfocused on selling and servicing customers while spending little time developing their people, leading, training, setting up systems, and planning.

## A WORD ON TIME MANAGEMENT

Time management seems to fill many books, and you've probably read one or two, so I'm sure you'll want to say, "I already know this stuff." But I can guarantee that even if you know it, you're not practicing it. How do I know this? Because I know it all and I don't practice it all! It takes a lifetime to master time management, and then the game changes because the tools and technologies change. Some of you learned Microsoft Outlook or Act! Then a decade went by, and now there are a dozen other programs to choose from to manage your time. Does anyone remember Franklin Covey planners or Day Runners? Those are tools of the past; most people don't use them anymore.

What am I going to say that is different than what all the other experts have said? Well, the answer is probably nothing, something, and everything.

I can tell you that if you want to grow your business and yourself, you will have to change your relationship to this subject.

When we say, "I know that!"—trust me, I think it more often than I care to admit!—you are preventing any further growth on that subject. You're telling the universe there's nothing further to learn or do. You're already doing it all. And I can practically guarantee that this is the furthest thing from the truth. You're not doing it all, so stop lying to yourself.

First, to become a great time manager, you need to have some structured understanding of the subject and some mental toughness. You'll have to bring energy, enthusiasm, and excitement to the endeavor.

Let's start with structured understanding. You'll need to accept that we all have the same amount of time and that the only way to get more time is to work more, sleep less, and take time away from other things such as hobbies and family time. Or you can try to combine them creatively. For example, you work more and do it with family members so you're talking work over lunch, at the golf course, and up the chairlift on the ski mountain. You get the picture. Working more is an excellent recipe for burnout, and sleeping less makes it likely that you will not be making decisions with a clear mind.

## TIME MANAGEMENT REDEFINED IS PRIORITY MANAGEMENT

There's a famous hundred-year-old story from 1918 when Ivy Lee, a productivity consultant, was hired by Charles M. Schwab, the president of Bethlehem Steel Corporation, to improve his company's efficiency. Lee's method was to work only with the top executives and have them write down each night their six most important tasks to accomplish the next day. The next day, he'd have them work on the tasks one at a time until they were completed. And repeat each night. As the story goes, Lee offered his method to Schwab for free, telling him to pay him what he thought it was worth. After three months, Schwab was so pleased with the results that he wrote Lee a check for $25,000—the equivalent of $425,000 today!

You'll need to understand that with a finite amount of time, you have to focus on the critical things. This is essential to time management. By prioritizing your to-do list, you get to focus on what matters most, which is where mental toughness comes into play. To say yes to some activities, you must say no to others, which requires discipline and focus. It reminds me of something I heard spoken by Brian Tracy. He suggested that we ask ourselves more than once a day, "What is the most important thing I can be doing right now?"

Saying no more often so that we can focus on the vital work is the key. I have taken hundreds of business owners through an exercise called the Vital Few/Trivial Many, and it's incredible how well it has worked with people who are open-minded, coachable, and willing to change. By the way, it's also amazing how poorly it's worked with people who are closed-off and invested in staying the same.

When I first started my group coaching practice in 2004, every ninety days I would take a group of small business owners offsite to a golf course, hotel, or meeting room for a full-day workshop. One of the exercises was to have them complete a worksheet on their Vital Few/Trivial Many activities. Those whose worlds were changing would get remarkable results from repeating this exercise. Those whose worlds were not changing would tell me they got the same answers they got last time.

Jake Nonnemaker, the owner of a small, family-run IT services company, was one of my first clients at these workshops. Before participating in my all-day workshop, the first in a series held every quarter with the same people, Jake could not imagine taking a day off from work to focus on his business. After attending the first workshop, he told anyone who would listen to him that if they didn't feel they could take a day off, this workshop was exactly what they needed.

This is what he shared after taking the series of workshops:

*Jonathan Goldhill and his programs are directly responsible for increasing the revenue of my company by over 50%. His techniques and methods have allowed me to focus clearly on my goals and remove the obstacles that were preventing me from achieving my goals. The improvements in my business were realized almost immediately after implementing his techniques. My company has been in business for over nine years, but the last few years were spent in a rut. Sales would go up and down, but there wasn't any consistent upward movement. Jonathan showed me how to make changes in my business and to break out of that stagnant cycle. We are now producing consistent results, and my company is growing once again. My wife says she hasn't seen me so energized in years and has noted a distinct improvement in my business attitude, confidence, and energy. Jonathan brings a lot of real-life experience and practical knowledge to the table.*

—JAKE, CEO, AXICOM

The key to the Vital Few/Trivial Many exercise is to discriminate between those activities that are vital to your role in the business and those tasks that are trivial. The key is to commit to strategies for doing more of the Vital Few and to decide what you will do with the Trivial Many. Will you do, delete, delegate, redesign, or outsource these tasks?

I have found this exercise works well with leaders who need to see the value of hiring someone, whether they be full time, part time, fractional, or outsourced, to take over some or even many of the tasks that the leader should not be doing themselves. By working on trivial tasks, leaders are taking time away from the vital few activities that really will propel the business.

Chris Lonergan is the disruptive successor, owner, and CEO of two businesses founded by his father, Doug Lonergan. One is a benefits administration software and the other a full-service marketing communications firm specializing in HR and benefit-related deliverables. He has found that this one exercise repeated quarterly has helped him elevate himself and delegate lesser essential activities. During our first year of working together, we hired two presidents—one to run each company. Since then, he has been able to focus on what he is most passionate about: sales and business development. With skilled, proven leaders running each company, he has positioned the businesses to grow.

So if you want to grow your business, you and other members of your family and team will need to replace yourselves in the jobs that don't highlight your value to the company. Think about it. Suddenly, time management is now money management. If you are worth $400,000/year and work forty hours/week, fifty weeks/year, then your hourly rate is $200/hour. But if you are doing $50/hour work, then you are stealing $150/hour for every hour you do that work. You're also forgoing an hour of truly important work OR working an extra hour.

Think about that, and you'll probably think twice about Brian Tracy's question, "What is the most valuable use of my time right now?" Focus on staying in your strengths zone; otherwise, you'll be doing work that saps your energy, too!

Multitasking is another issue. There has been a lot of debate on this subject, and I believe the verdict is final. Multitasking is not practical. Think about it.

Limit multitasking. As my coach once said to me, think of "focus" as an acronym that stands for Follow One Course Until Successful. FOCUS. When I sat down to write this book, I eliminated all distractions—emails, phone calls, client work—and that enabled me to get my rough draft done in record time. When I did my rewrites after my editor's review, I allowed the above interruptions, thus dragging out the process of finishing the book for months.

After more than thirty years sitting in the offices of CEOs, presidents, and owners, I have observed the behaviors of some of the most successful individuals and some of the most dysfunctional ones. It's a no-brainer that the highly dysfunctional ones are always allowing interruptions, micromanaging too many people's jobs, and juggling family, friends, customers, employees, and the consultant sitting opposite them. That consultant was me in my earlier days, and I was too kind, young, and inexperienced to get the person to stop their insanity. Their multitasking was killing them. They might have been getting stuff done, but they were always having to redo and undo hasty and poorly made decisions, with no thought to ending the firefighting.

## ENERGY MANAGEMENT

Poor decisions may be a sign of stupidity, but they are more often a sign of inadequate energy management. By energy management, I mean physical fitness, mental fitness, emotional fitness, and similar things that help you to control your well-being, which takes me to another subject: your brain chemistry is crucial to your vitality and your business's health.

If we manage our energy, state of being, thoughts, bodies, emotions, and spirits (and I don't mean alcohol), we will bring enthusiasm to the work at hand. Passion will drive us to work more effectively (doing the right work) and efficiently (doing the work right), which in the end will give us more time to spend with our family, friends, hobbies, and more.

Let's get back to your understanding of time management. There are a few rules I'd like to suggest as best practices for planning your day. First, every day set at most five to six main goals that consume about two-thirds of the day. Your calendar should have two to three hours of unscheduled time in each day to allow for unexpected activities, interruptions, client or customer calls, employee issues, and so forth. The bulk of your day should be planned and input into a calendar (I recommend that if others have access to your schedule, you indicate your free time so that others see when you are available). The key is that you must tackle your most important priorities first.

That's where Brian Tracy came up with the term and title to his book *Eat That Frog* because the way to eat a frog is to eat the biggest, ugliest piece first, in one bite if possible, to get it over with.

Suppose you must fire someone. Nobody likes firing people. When you have to fire someone, maybe that's the first thing you do that day. It gives you a chance, assuming you're well rested and calmest in the morning, to do it with care and empathy.

Brendon Burchard, the *High Performance Habits* guy, has a tool I like called the 1-Page Productivity Planner. It's an elegantly laid-out one-sheet of your Projects, People, and Priorities. The Projects section has a place to list the five big things you must do to move each of your projects forward. The People section has two boxes: one for the people you need to reach out to today and the other for the people you're waiting on to move something forward. The Priorities section is for the things you must complete today, no matter what. Your goal in priority management is to make the main thing your number-one thing. That means focus on the activity with the most potential to move your business forward. FOCUS. Learn to say no. Saying no to something means you're saying yes to something else. Focus on your priorities so your big items get done first. Don't get caught up in your inbox (like I do!) or on trivial activities.

## SETTING PRIORITIES REQUIRES PROPER PLANNING

If you spend more time planning your business, you will see magical results. Your planning process can either start with the present day or with the end goal. If you prefer the latter, plan as far ahead as you can. For most people, that's three to five years, but a few rare individuals have a ten- to twenty-five-year vision. Most people overestimate what they can do in that time frame and underestimate what they can do in the next ninety days.

For many people, planning every ninety days is a good rhythm. I like to work with my clients every week so that they are not just planning every ninety days but also setting weekly actions with an eye on the ninety-day goals. Every ninety days, we meet in person to plan out our quarterly, annual, and three- to five-year goals. It's much easier to set your priorities when you have a longer-term vision and know what the prize at the end is.

In addition to quarterly team meetings and weekly one-on-one meetings, I recommend that my clients have a daily huddle with their team and that the other teams in the company have daily huddles, too. These are five- to fifteen-minute check-ins where people share what they're working on today, how they did yesterday, and where they may be stuck. This way, everyone is staying on track and is accountable for any daily metrics the company may be tracking.

I also encourage my clients to have weekly and monthly team meetings with their staff. The weekly and monthly meetings ensure the entire team is working toward their quarterly priorities and measuring their activities against carefully chosen metrics and performance indicators.

I find that most teams need to learn some of the basics of how to manage their time more effectively. Typically, I recommend they read an easy-to-read book on the subject to get them on the path toward becoming more productive. Usually, they need some training, too. Training allows them to ask questions and develop their best time-management practices because what works best is what they will use most often.

I use my calendar to manage all my activities. I color-code it to make sure I have a balance of activities (exercise, client work, writing time, and free time).

For others, keeping three master lists of tasks work better. They keep a cumulative to-do list. On their Vital Few/Trivial Many, they're holding a "not-to-do" list. Then they also have their daily to-dos, which they can put into their calendar each day or each week. Most follow my recommendation of labeling each block in their schedule as free time, busy, or out-of-office task.

To keep it simple, I prefer to use Microsoft Outlook. I use Evernote for ideas, notes, and other to-do lists, but these programs change all the time, and people are often moving from one to another depending on their facility with applications.

For setting longer-term goals and priorities, my clients use a variety of applications. Some use software programs I recommend (e.g., Traction Tools and Metronome Growth Systems) that allow their entire team to see the business plan, metrics, and priorities of each teammate. Some prefer to use a cloud-based or shared drive, such as Google Drive.

One essential thing, which the older crowd often overlooks, is that everything should be in a digital format so that it's accessible universally. It does you no good to have a paper calendar anymore since you can't access it remotely, and neither can others.

I have seen the techniques presented in this chapter work so well in my life and my clients'. I believe that if time and priority management were the only thing I did for my clients, I could have a phenomenally successful business. It's that significant.

I've used it to focus my lifestyle business on what I have to accomplish today, this week, and this quarter. I've witnessed client after client continue to redefine their roles and priorities every ninety days so that they are learning, growing, and finding more fulfillment.

Everyone can learn to better manage their time, priorities, and energy. So keep reinvesting in learning for yourself and your team. The result will be that everyone gets on the same page (literally) and aligns with the same priorities.

Next, let's talk about building a great team, because it's more than your family that you'll be depending on.

## ACTION STEPS

1. Organize your life (health, fitness, diet, sleep, distractions, etc.) to achieve maximum energy. Get help from an accountability partner, friend, health/fitness coach, and so on.
2. Identify your priorities and coach your team to identify theirs. Develop them regularly in your quarterly meetings and review your progress in your monthly meetings. Manage against them in your daily and weekly priority management system—for example, your calendar.
3. Either plan your priorities backward—from lifetime to annual to quarterly to monthly to weekly to daily—or do it forward from today to the future. Imagine your goals happening to help you manifest their achievement.

# CHAPTER 10

# PRIORITIES

## ACCOUNTABILITY, RESPONSIBILITY, AUTHORITY, AND OWNERSHIP

*"Responsibility equals accountability equals ownership. And a sense of ownership is the most powerful weapon a team or organization can have."*

—PAT SUMMITT, AMERICAN WOMEN'S COLLEGE BASKETBALL COACH WITH MOST CAREER WINS UPON HER RETIREMENT

Many businesses suffer because of a partial or total lack of accountability. In a family business, accountability means being held responsible by the family and the company. When accountability is missing in a family business, a pervasive attitude of entitlement may be the cause. When entitlement is present in a family business, it can lead to the demise of the company and undoing of family bonds.

Accountability hyperactivity deficit disorder is a problem at many companies where their behaviors, at one extreme, are reminiscent of Keystone Cops from the silent movie days. These companies are typically led by an entrepreneur who has mild to severe ADD (attention deficit disorder, now more commonly referred to as ADHD, or attention deficit hyperactivity disorder). The worse their ADD/ADHD, the worse the accountability deficit disorder is in the business. Like when the CEO comes into the office fresh from their latest peer group meeting or personal growth workshop or business workshop and wants to implement the new thing they just learned. Sound familiar?

These ailments are rampant among entrepreneurs, perhaps because so many of us have some tendencies of the other ADD/ADHD, which is what got us started on the entrepreneurial path to begin with. Those issues take time to overcome, usually with the help of an outside therapist, consultant, or coach, or in some cases, medicine. Left uncorrected, they can be fatal to the long-term sustainability of any business.

Because the family business environment is fundamentally more inclusive, more unconditional, and more informal, accountability deficit disorder can be especially prevalent. That's because we tend to be less stern with our family members.

If you are going to scale your company and lead it through an intergenerational transition, you will need tools, systems, and processes to hold your people accountable.

You don't need the best talent in every position (although it helps); you need good people who follow sound systems developed by other good people. Having a culture of accountability in your company will be natural if you have the right leaders because great leaders thrive in such a culture.

You must work to instill this new culture because it's likely a radical departure from that of the founder. You have ambitious goals and aspirations for significant growth—ones you can only achieve with people who understand the distinctions between responsibility, accountability, authority, and ownership.

## CREATE A CULTURE OF ACCOUNTABILITY

Let's start with how to create a culture of accountability. A culture of accountability develops when people take "ownership" of activities, commitments, and the measures they report on.

For instance, the VP of sales and marketing might be responsible for a measure like the total number of sales leads generated and closed. He might be accountable for the results, but it may not be his fault that the company didn't achieve its goals this past month/quarter/year. Perhaps the lack of sales was due to factors beyond his control, such as the economy or the market or lack of available dollars to experiment with different marketing activities.

Accountability also refers to "ownership" of assignments, initiatives, priorities, and projects measured qualitatively rather than quantitatively. Typically, these are marked as "complete" or "incomplete."

For example, consider the installation of new CRM software; in our company, the best practice is to take such a complicated assignment and break it down into steps or phases so that progress can be measured along the way. Often, when complex projects or assignments take multiple weeks, we break them down step by step and report to the group weekly on our progress toward completion. When done right, this is real accountability.

We create a culture of accountability through our actions.

- We walk our talk.
- We define results and expectations up front.
- We commit to the intended results by requiring people hold each other accountable to them.
- We stay open to feedback and problem solving around activities, commitments, and measures.
- We coach each other on how to be accountable.
- We use consequences and reinforcement to maintain a culture of accountability.

## ACCOUNTABILITY VERSUS RESPONSIBILITY VERSUS OWNERSHIP VERSUS AUTHORITY

Frequently, clients will ask me what the difference between accountability and responsibility is. The main difference is that responsibility can be shared whereas accountability cannot. Being accountable not only means being responsible but ultimately having to answer for your actions.

You can be accountable and responsible without having authority. In the example above, where the VP of sales and marketing was both accountable and responsible, the owner would probably have the ultimate authority.

A company where people hold each other accountable is a great company to work for and with. Priorities and goals are clearly understood, and people are more easily called out when they aren't accountable. There is no wiggle room or ambiguity around agreements, and people are happier when what needs to get done is done on time.

Companies that don't hold people accountable or fail to have the right metrics in place are often in disarray. There are frequent "fire drills," sometimes even fighting, finger-pointing, and a culture of victimhood. In these companies, leaders vent to me that they just don't know if a certain person is doing his/her job or not. This is not only frustrating to the leader but also to that person's teammates and subordinates.

Let's look at an example. One of my clients was the founder, along with his brother, of a digital signage company with a unique retail application in furniture stores and the potential to disrupt the brick-and-mortar furniture business. When this company's head of engineering kept his team protected from the rest of the leaders, the CEO didn't know whether he was defending himself or his team. So I counseled the CEO on using his authority to hold the department head accountable for the activities and measures that the group was responsible for completing. And when the CEO's brother wasn't performing the duties of a chief technology officer (CTO) as effectively as expected, the CEO had to use his authority to speak with his brother about this. Even though the brother has some shared ownership in the business, the CEO had the authority to hold him accountable for performing his duties as CTO.

To create a culture of accountability in a family business, hire people who enjoy taking initiative and responsibility. Set clear and measurable goals. Employees and family members who relish accountability will welcome the challenge of meeting expectations. Delegate authority and responsibility; push it down the organization as far as possible. The more power and shared ownership within the lower ranks, the more you will be freed up to work on higher-impact, higher-priority, and more-challenging activities. Measure and review your results regularly and address deficiencies. Help people when they are stuck, whether they are a family member, teammate, subordinate, or superior.

When you explicitly communicate goals and standards of behavior and regularly evaluate performance against them, you build a culture of accountability. You and your teammates need to call each other out and be prepared to be called out when you don't achieve what you set out to do. This form of public recognition (or lack of it) has a gentle but powerful way of making sure people stay in line with a focus on the outcome.

Holding family members accountable can be tricky because your judgment can be clouded by your relationship outside the business. Still, it's essential to maintain clarity on the role you are playing in the company to maintain the consistency the business requires. You are the leader. You can have authority if you earn it.

## THE WHO-WHAT-WHEN TO-DO LIST

We all have our to-do lists, but too few companies track individual commitments on a company to-do list. In the process of working together, we come up with many small tasks that need to be captured and recorded—and not in a document created with minutes of a meeting, which nobody is going to read. These immediate actions or commitments should be recorded onto a to-do list form I call the Who-What-When (WWW). This form spells out who will do what by when. Pretty simple, but it's amazing how many teams get this tool wrong!

Using it religiously is a small but consistent method of building a culture of accountability. Nobody likes to sit in meeting after meeting, week after week, and hear again about how some activity was not completed well.

## DELEGATION VERSUS ABDICATION

Just because you don't have time to teach someone how to do something doesn't mean that you should delegate it to them without any instructions. That's abdication. This action will set them up to fail, which is ultimately a failure on your end.

As a leader or owner, accountability starts with you. Responsibility and accountability can and should be delegated to others, but only after you demonstrate how accountable you are to a set of standards, values, behaviors, and so forth. Your people are looking to you as the model example. You must walk the talk. You must hold people accountable. And the people beneath you must hold the people beneath them accountable.

Accountability is usually the difference between success and failure.

## ACTION STEP

1. Visit www.DisruptiveSuccessor.com website and download the WWW To-Do List tool.

## CHAPTER 11

# PRIORITIES

## MEETINGS KEEP US FOCUSED ON OUR PRIORITIES

*"The majority of meetings should be discussions that lead to decisions."*

—PATRICK LENCIONI, AUTHOR OF BUSINESS BOOKS

Meetings are probably the most maligned subject in the world of business. But that's because they are poorly designed and poorly managed. It's been said that meetings have such a bad reputation that most people think of politicians as people who get nothing done because all they do is go to meetings.

Some say that they have too many meetings already and don't want any more. I would argue that most of their meetings probably are not that effective or that they're not holding the right types of meetings. So, in this chapter, I will not only discuss why you should hold meetings, but also what these meetings should be, when to have them, and how to make decisions in them.

Although family meetings are often seen as complicated, they are critical to:

- Building trust
- Resolving conflict
- Decision making
- Creating unity
- Encouraging innovation
- Facilitating alignment to a shared strategic vision

However, there are times when family differences expose a lack of trust that has resulted in fake harmony among family members. When family members lack faith in each other, their different opinions must be expressed in the safe setting of a structured meeting in order to surface the hidden conflicts and try to work through them to restore harmony and trust. That said, I have worked with more than one family business where it was impossible to restore trust because there was too much emotional damage done over the years.

One of the biggest problems common to many businesses, family or otherwise, is that meetings are not effectively and efficiently run and fail to communicate what's going on in the company or the industry. In a business of any size, sharing knowledge with your leaders and managers builds their capacity. Meetings are essential times to discuss delicate items and facilitate alignment on things such as vision, direction, strategies, priorities, and to-dos. Regular meetings allow you to move faster; break down the walls between people and departments that lead to silos, politics, and turf wars; and improve focus on the goals and create alignment to the business plan.

Regular meetings run right will help to:

- Provide problem-solving opportunities
- Make fast adjustments and course corrections

- Eliminate communication gaps
- Break down complexities as the company grows
- Align the leadership team, the family, and the employees

So often in a family business, family members spend a lot of time with each other but don't discuss all of the issues. Blind spots in their communication go ignored, and sensitive items don't get addressed because they might upset the homeostasis of the business.

Frequently, the thinking is, "We're family and we discuss everything." But do you? Or are you blinded by the fact that you are family and avoiding the problematic stuff that will take heavy lifting to change? In smaller family businesses, leaders are in discussions with each other so often that the interruptions, rather than the company's priorities, become the focus.

In a family business, there is often a tendency to get sidetracked. The dynamics at play are complicated, and familiarity can stand in the way of getting things done.

Take, for example, a firm run by several family members, including extended family. On the plus side, each stakeholder is hugely engaged in the business; their lives revolve around it. However, they have little in the way of systems, so they are very disorganized, and on most days, chaos rules. What sustains them is that they're always together and talking about the business. They put an incredible amount of energy into what they do, but they just can't seem to get ahead.

What they need are systems. They lack structure, so their progress is inconsistent. They do a lot of talking and discuss many things, but they aren't focused on what's important.

There is an illusion that a lot is getting done, but the opposite is the case.

The answer—or at least the gateway to a solution—is to establish a meeting schedule, which I'll get to in a moment.

First, let's go over some tips for having productive meetings.

## TIPS FOR ESTABLISHING AN EFFECTIVE MEETING PROCESS

Here are a few tips for creating productive meetings:

- Set the dates for your annual, quarterly, and monthly meetings a year in advance.
- Communicate with all stakeholders and check in often.
- Be fully prepared before walking into a meeting.
- Don't lose sight of what you are responsible for. Take notes on decisions and critical issues only, stay focused, and be accountable for the agenda and process.
- Maintain meeting structure. The less structured your meetings are, the less effective they will be.
- Hire a facilitator to make sure valuable items are discussed. That way, you can participate fully and not have to manage the process.

I recommend you start by holding productive leadership team meetings so leaders see the value in well-conceived and productive meetings. Then encourage your department managers to begin holding meetings with their teams, continuing to cascade these meetings down until everyone is participating in a daily huddle. Sometimes these huddles are done company-wide. Schedule the meetings such that team leaders can participate in both their department team's meeting and their leadership team meeting.

Suppose you own a construction company that has five departments: design, commercial installation, residential installation, maintenance, and repairs. You might want to participate in each department's meetings so that you are aware of each one's workload. Attending these will give you a full view of the company and lessen the likelihood of silos. It also lets you know how you might assist or get support from other team leaders. And it helps you coordinate resources, review progress, and make decisions that are specific to a particular team. By staggering meeting start times, you can attend more team meetings as needed. Cascading start times gives you an opportunity to synchronize your daily activities with those of other leaders in the company.

The default agenda for your weekly and monthly meetings should be pretty much the same each week and month; these are times to work through issues the group needs to solve. Each week, you and the team should identify what problems or priorities you'll address in the weekly meeting. Prioritize your topics and keep a parking lot of issues to choose from each session. Send any materials in advance so people are prepared.

You may decide to discuss why you are falling short of individual goals. You may brainstorm ways for a department facing challenges to solve them. You might discuss a strategic issue or some feedback from customers or employees. It's essential to keep the conversation fresh, meaning you don't deal with the same problems repeatedly. Have someone play referee when the conversation strays from the subject at hand. Stay focused. Solve the issue, and then move on to another if there's time.

Be careful not to solve problems prematurely. It's a common mistake to try to solve a problem before correctly diagnosing it. When you do this, the problem comes back rearing its ugly head only a few weeks or months later. The best way to diagnose a problem is to use a form of appreciative inquiry where you ask questions of the person presenting the problem. Let them answer everybody's questions before you start solving the problem. Inevitably, there will be one person who likes to solve other people's issues without knowing the full situation. Make sure all the pertinent information is out on the table before the team addresses a problem.

## SHOW UP ON TIME AND COME PREPARED

Another best practice for holding meetings is to make sure they start and end on time. Everyone has calendars and appointments to handle. It's best to set and follow an agenda with a specific start and end time. Give people a warning when you're nearing the end and suggest which agenda items should be held over until the next meeting. Or, if some are urgent, set an ad hoc meeting for another time.

## NOTE TAKING

Taking detailed notes isn't necessary because most people will never review them. Have a note taker keep track of action items only. Have them put things to be discussed later in the parking lot list. Light note taking focused on decisions and action is especially useful to show those absent what was covered and what will be covered in an upcoming meeting. We often refer to the WWW (Who, What, When), the single document that captures short-term actions and commitments made. If everyone stays mentally and physically present, you won't need notes. People will remember what was said.

## HAVE A FULL SET OF RULES

1. Start on time; end on time.
2. Foster healthy conflict.
3. Attack problems, not people.
4. No electronics (unless otherwise agreed upon).
5. Silence = agreement.
6. No sidebars—be fully present.
7. Scout rule: be prepared.
8. Vegas rule: what happens in the meeting stays in the meeting if it's private.
9. Stay on topic: parking lot issues for later discussion.
10. Accountability—do what we say we're going to do.
11. No elephants or sacred cows: we won't avoid a critical topic because it's sensitive.

An essential tool you will need for the meeting is your calendar. People too often don't have their schedules with them and waste time negotiating appointments. Even if your company is large enough that your scheduling secretaries will handle this, why tax them with back-and-forth emailing to get dates set on the calendar?

## MAKE MEETINGS INTERESTING

If you want to make your meetings compelling, involve some sharing of personal and professional news. Make the meetings current so people can become present in the room and with each other. If someone is dealing with something significant in their personal life, they'll feel heard if they can share their circumstances and state of mind. It just makes people feel comfortable.

I recommend doing some team exercises that help members bond with and understand each other. I do an activity with nonfamily members called a lifeline exercise that has them share their personal life histories from childhood to present. In this exercise, you graph your history, showing high points and low points, then share them with the group. It's an opportunity to get comfortable with each other and appreciate each other's unique backgrounds.

## MAKE MEETINGS COUNT

People can struggle to find good times to meet with other members of their team. In my experience, there is no best time to schedule meetings. Some say mornings are best because you are fresh and alert. Others say they have other things to do in the morning and that later in the day is better. Others say afternoons are best but not too late. The fact is that you should try to find a time that is mutually agreeable to all and stick with it unless it's not working. Maybe let one person pick the time for three months and another pick the time for another three months. Be consistent, but try different times.

The day of the week will matter to some. I like Mondays because you can plan for the whole workweek. Others like Fridays because they can reflect on what got done that week and what still needs to get done. Wednesday can be a great day for a meeting because you're partway into the week; you can look ahead to the next week while still having a few days to course correct your efforts.

Bottom line: It doesn't matter. What matters is that you are meeting on a regular and recurring basis. It's the consistency and the practices that matter.

## ESTABLISH A MEETING RHYTHM AND AGENDA

Typically, meeting rhythm consists of daily, weekly, monthly, quarterly, and annual meetings, each one with a particular purpose and structure to optimize its utility and effectiveness.

### 1. THE DAILY HUDDLE

The daily huddle, which should take no more than ten to fifteen minutes, is the time for each team to quickly discuss what's coming up that day, what people might need help with, and any measures of productivity from the previous day. It's a way of getting organized with each other, not merely a recitation of your calendar for that day. I recommend that these daily huddles start at an odd time—for example, 9:07 a.m.—so that it's not forgotten and is treated differently from all the other meetings.

Here's how you could structure your huddle time:

| | |
|---|---|
| Personal/professional good news—wins since the previous meeting | (2–5 minutes) |
| Daily measures, if you have any | (2–5 minutes) |
| What's happening the next twenty-four hours | (2–5 minutes) |
| Your challenges—anything you are stuck on or need help with | (2–5 minutes) |

### 2. THE WEEKLY MEETING

Weekly meetings are held to share weekly progress toward quarterly goals and to solve tactical issues you need others' input on. These meetings are critical to accountability and making adjustments to your leadership strategy. The structure is much the same as the daily huddle but with a more long-range focus. Take sixty to ninety minutes to engage and focus your team.

On the agenda:

- Wins and other good news
- Company priorities
- Performance indicator updates
- Items that require immediate action
- What your customers and employees are saying

### 3. THE MONTHLY MEETING

The monthly meeting is a lot like the weekly meeting. It is also a time for team building, team learning, and discussion of strategic issues and opportunities. Depending on the size of your team, the monthly meeting might last a half day. It connects the management and executive teams for team building, problem solving, and learning.

Here's a recommended structure for your monthly meetings:

- Celebrate wins
- Updates on progress toward the quarterly goals
- Education and training on a specific leadership or technical skill
- Identify, discuss, and solve process or people issues

- Summing up, chart the path forward

## 4. THE QUARTERLY MEETING

The quarterly meeting is like the monthly meeting but longer. It is for reporting, reviewing, and resetting goals for the upcoming ninety days. It is an excellent opportunity to discuss broader issues such as staffing and personnel, organizational structure, systems and processes that are missing or need to be updated, financial considerations, and strategy/execution challenges. The quarterly session focuses on the leadership and management teams—probably separately—and their successes and struggles. Usually spread over a couple of days, it's a chance to establish a plan for the coming quarter.

On the agenda:

- Review and discuss issues since your last quarterly meeting
- Brainstorm ideas for growth and action
- Align strategy to action
- Plan how you will move forward
- Walk through the plan in hypotheticals
- Cascade planning
- Talk about how you will communicate and report your results

## 5. THE ANNUAL MEETING

The annual meeting is a two- to three-day session to strategize for the coming year. It provides a forum to set yearly targets, draft initiatives, establish your first-quarter plan, and decide how to cascade and communicate the mission to the rest of the company.

On the agenda:

- Review and discuss issues since your last quarterly meeting
- Brainstorm ideas for growth and action
- Align strategy to action
- Assess progress on your three- to five-year plan
- Execution plans for annual, quarterly, cascade, and communication

### 6. THE AD HOC MEETING

The ad hoc meeting is a meeting to discuss an issue that has surfaced and requires some time to discuss and solve.

Be careful: your ad hoc meetings may be too frequent if you aren't processing your problems in your other meetings. When ad hoc meetings are necessary, try to put a boundary around the time to process the issue—for example, thirty minutes—and the date by which it must be resolved—for example, Monday at 5:00 p.m.

When you step into an ad hoc meeting, suggest an agenda up front to avoid open-ended meetings with wandering discussions, clarify the issue, and process it using the Issue, Discuss, Recommendation model.

### 7. BIWEEKLY ONE-ON-ONE MEETINGS WITH MANAGERS

Everyone deserves a coach. As the leader of your company, you probably manage three to seven direct reports. Each of them needs and deserves coaching. One-on-one meetings are valuable opportunities to check in and connect with your direct reports, provide them with coaching and motivation, and be a resource to them. These should not be "command and control"-style meetings but opportunities for listening and providing guidance and feedback. If you have to command and control, then either you don't have a capable direct report or your style hasn't been updated to address the modern-day workforce. If you manage the ideal number of direct reports, five to seven people maximum, then these meetings can happen every week, biweekly, or monthly, as appropriate.

The conversation should be focused on seven simple questions:

1. How are you doing?
2. How is your team doing?
3. How are we doing?
4. What are you working on?
5. What can I help you with?
6. What tools and resources do you need?
7. Is there anything else?

Either you can hire a leadership team coach, like me, or you can run the meeting yourself. Either way, you will want to have a structured agenda to make the meeting easier to manage, keep it to about forty-five to fifty minutes, and cover some or all of the topics below (in the order below):

Here's a sample agenda:

| | |
|---|---|
| Check-in—personal and professional | (5 minutes) |
| Identify any hot topics to discuss | (2 minutes) |
| Individual (quarterly) priorities—progress | (10 minutes) |
| Projects you are working on and obstacles with them | (10 minutes) |
| Decisions you're facing and obstacles to making them | (10 minutes) |
| Review top tasks for last two-week meeting | (10 minutes) |
| Direct report review—effectiveness/issues | (10 minutes) |
| Annual goal/target review discussion | (10 minutes) |
| What else? | (5 minutes) |

## 8. THE ALL-HANDS MEETING

The all-hands meeting is like an executive report or "State of the Union." It is a regular company-wide gathering where leadership updates all employees on important activities and milestones of the business.

An agenda covering these five items might look like this:

1. Drive alignment around company vision, values, mission, strategy, and so forth.
2. Share business updates from the past month, quarter, or season and progress toward goals/initiatives
3. Reinforce the strategy, direction, priorities, and so forth.
4. Celebrate our results
5. Give everyone a chance to ask questions

## 9. THE FAMILY SHAREHOLDER MEETING

Families and shareholders (and they may be the same) should have regular meetings to review and discuss business and personal issues. A sample agenda might be:

- Buffet breakfast gathering
- Personal and professional check-ins
- Hot topics: family issues
- Review company financials results
- Review changes to the shareholder agreement, ownership, dividend, or other policies
- Review/discuss tax and estate issues
- Discuss family roadmap—that is, succession
- Shared learning activity
- Socialize

## 10. FAMILY BUSINESS MEETINGS

You need to seriously consider who will attend these meetings. Generally speaking, less is better. In family businesses, seven distinct constituencies must be considered when setting up a meeting schedule.

John Davis developed the Three-Circle Model of the Family Business System[18] in which he identified seven different stakeholder groups that show up in multigenerational family businesses.

## THREE-CIRCLE MODEL OF THE FAMILY BUSINESS SYSTEM

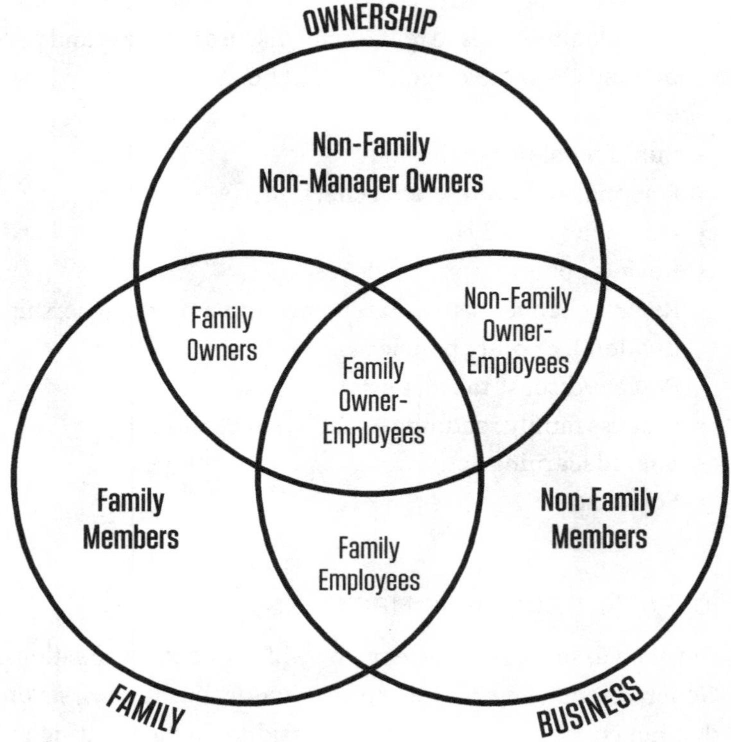


© Tagiuri and Davis 1982

The seven groups are:

1. Family owner-employees in the business
2. Family owners not in the business
3. Nonfamily owner-employees in the business
4. Family employees who are not owners
5. Nonfamily, non-manager owners not in the business
6. Family members not in the business
7. Nonfamily members in the business

Typically, a family meeting or family council is established to represent these seven different constituencies and meets annually in an informal, almost casual fashion to discuss transition and succession.

## FAMILY DYNAMICS: THE MARKSON FAMILY CONSTRUCTION BUSINESS STORY

As you may recall, Markson Contracting is in a bit of a pickle. The patriarch of the company is in poor health and has stepped back from the day-to-day. He expects his three sons to share equally in running the family business.

Lacking leadership and oversight, the personalities of the three working Markson sons overshadow just about everything they do. The brothers do their best to get through each day without killing each other or walking away. But if they do not alter their approach, the outcome is not going to be a good one.

As owners, family, and employees, the three Markson brothers share the same role. On the Three-Circle Model, they all live at the very core of the business—the center of the diagram—and it's not working. No blood is flowing to the other segments of the circles, and the company is suffering because of it.

What the Three-Circle Model tells us is that if any one segment has conflict, it will bring down the rest. Progress and development will stall out, and the whole system will collapse—that's where the Markson family business stands right now.

## FAMILY BUSINESS CONFLICTS: HOW DIFFERENT ROLES AFFECT THE WHOLE

1. **The Founder:** Having retired, Markson Sr. is removed from the middle section of the model. He is family and owner but no longer an employee. He does not have the influence over the operation that he once did, but his presence is still felt.
2. **The Spouse:** Mrs. Markson is family, she does not work for the company, and she is not an owner per se, but she does have influence. Despite the raging conflict the brothers experience each day, Mrs. Markson manages to keep their relationships from imploding completely. According to her, the family business is riding on the three boys carrying out their father's wishes. The sons do their best to hide what is going on from her.
3. **Nonfamily Employees:** They are used to constant conflict. As a result, they do not communicate well with any of the Markson family. Details are missed, timelines are overshot, and projects are not managed efficiently. There is a lack of engagement and accountability.

## HOW COULD THIS SITUATION HAVE BEEN DIFFERENT?

When Markson Sr. was in his prime, he ran a tight ship. Eric was his right hand for many years, but the younger man was always under his father's thumb and rarely allowed to think for himself. To keep Eric engaged, Markson Sr. would frequently say, "This will be yours one day." That promise kept him going.

When Markson Sr. decided to have the three sons run the company equally, there was some understandable resentment on Eric's part. Having been the object of his father's scrutiny and criticism for many years, he is now taking it out on his younger brothers, whom he feels have not paid their dues.

The younger brothers are at first defensive and become resentful over time, often engaging in stonewalling behavior and creating an imbalance that spills over into all aspects of business operations.

So what went wrong?

Markson Sr.'s idea to bring the brothers together was not a bad one. On paper, at least, the three have complementary skills, and between them, they've got what it takes for the business to thrive.

What the company has now is one brother who felt like he was owed something and two who, for all their talents, don't have much skin in the family legacy.

Without leadership and guidance, the brothers have defaulted to what they know how to do. For the sake of their mother and out of loyalty to their father, they are trying to make it work. But with conflicting ideas about whose way is best, there is no chance for progress.

Unless they can look beyond the jealousy, the rage, the guilt, and their egos, there won't be much left to fight over. Although it's too late to change what's already happened with the Marksons, there is a way forward. It will take some work, but it's possible. It is never too late to improve your family business.

### ACTION STEPS

1. Set up your five to nine meetings and get them into the right people's calendars.
2. Create a default agenda for each of your meetings. For assistance with this, visit our Resources section of www.DisruptiveSuccessor.com and download Default Meeting Agendas.
3. Keep notes on the action items only. Create a WWW for short-term commitments. Log longer-term commitments, goals, priorities, and strategic thinking items on your One-Page Business Plan. Download samples from the Resources section of the www.DisruptiveSuccessor.com.

CHAPTER 12

# PROCESSES

## BUILD GREAT SYSTEMS TO SHORTEN THE PATH TO ANY GOAL

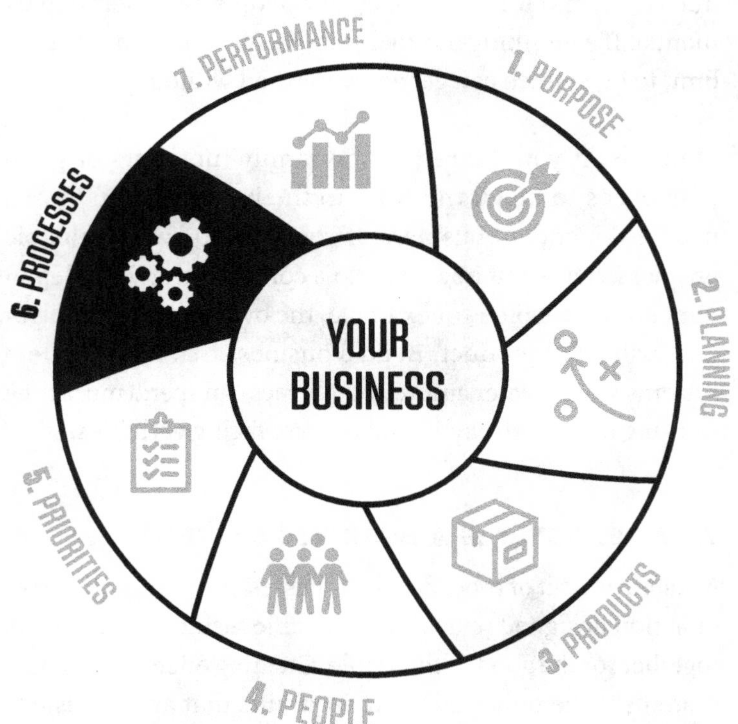

*"Organize around business functions, not people. Build systems within each business function. Let systems run the business, and people run the systems. People come and go, but the systems remain constant."*

—MICHAEL GERBER, AUTHOR OF *THE E MYTH*

Want to build a company that's fun to own and worth a fortune when you exit it? Then put systems in your business—the right systems. Superior systems improve the chances that your business can be managed or taken over by another person, which makes it more sellable and, thus, more valuable.

Imagine your business is like the wheel of a bicycle. It has a hub (you), and it has spokes (your people and their departments). If everything has to flow through you, then there is a limit to how much can get accomplished without you.

Similarly, if you are relying on family members or great employees to do all the work in the business, you have a people-dependent business. If you want to own a valuable business, figure out how to build a company that isn't dependent on key people—for example, the owner—to sell, deliver, and install the product. Build a business that has excellent systems so the owner and key employees can spend more time working on higher-payoff and market-facing activities.

## WHAT EXACTLY IS A BUSINESS SYSTEM?

A system is a set of procedures, processes, methods, or courses of action designed to achieve a specific result. Its parts work together for the good of the whole. Creating effective business systems is the only way to attain results that are consistent, measurable, and beneficial to customers.

A business system can be as simple as a checklist, which you can create in several easy steps. First, outline the high-level activities and a handful of subtasks. Next, detail the subtasks preferably in writing, but consider video if it makes the learning or teaching of the subtask more impactful. Finally, share the list so that others can use it and verify its accuracy.

If the system cuts across multiple departments, strategic business units, or people, consider drawing out a flowchart to illustrate the path it takes along with the intersecting tracks performed by other people.

## FIVE REASONS YOU NEED SYSTEMS

**Systems provide consistency.** When you have business systems in place, vital activities are teachable and can be replicated consistently by others. Hiring, firing, onboarding, selling, training, and so forth will have consistency, which will improve your business processes and ultimately increase profitability.

**Change is easier to accomplish.** When systems are documented, changes are easy to make. If systems are in the form of flowcharts or written series of sequential tasks, they can be easily modified. Video documentation is more difficult, of course, but still doable.

**Training employees is easier with systems.** Training employees, especially new hires, becomes simpler with documented procedures in place.

**Systems encourage employees to focus on what they do best.** Key employees can focus on knowledge-based activities that require executive reasoning skills and leave more routine activities to employees better suited to those.

**Systems create value.** If you ever want to sell or transition to a new owner or manager, formal procedures will add value to your business. A buyer will be more eager to purchase a company when it's a company that runs smoothly because the operations of the business are sound.

## WHAT SYSTEMS DO YOU NEED TO SCALE?

Essentially, you need systems for every significant process in the business and probably for the minor ones, too:

- Lead generation (Marketing)
- Lead conversion (Selling)
- Recordkeeping (Accounting)
- Making/buying (Producing)
- Delivering (Distribution)
- People management (Recruiting, hiring, managing people)
- Customer service
- Pricing (Estimating)
- Purchasing and procurement (Supply chain management)
- Business development (Partnering)

The key to documenting a business system is going to be unique to each business. You should start by identifying a handful of the most critical processes and documenting them in pictures, flowcharts, video tutorials, or written directions.

The best systems are those that are the most straightforward. It would be ideal if you didn't need instructions on how things worked, but in my experience, this isn't possible. It's interesting to note that Apple makes products that are so simple they don't come with instructions. But I don't know of any businesses that run well without them.

## WHAT SHOULD YOUR SYSTEM LOOK LIKE?

Suppose you are documenting your accounting system. You might have it broken down into four steps if you want to keep it very high level and super simple, or you might have it broken down into twelve steps for a more robust set of descriptions. Here are six reasonably high-level steps:

1. Analyzing the transactions as they occur
2. Recording them in journals
3. Posting debits and credits from journal entries to the general ledger
4. Adjusting the assets with a trial balance
5. Preparing financial statements
6. Closing the temporary accounts

Although that gives you the flow of the system, it doesn't go into enough detail on each step. But if everyone working within that system knows what to do, then you probably need to go further at this time in documenting the process.

In developing your systems, follow Occam's razor, the problem-solving principle attributed to the fourteenth-century philosopher William of Occam, that essentially states, "Simpler solutions are more likely to be correct than complex ones." In other words, in explaining a thing, make no more assumptions than are necessary.

## TEACH SYSTEM DEVELOPMENT

One of the simplest ways to teach people how to work a system is to use the master-apprentice model (see below).

### MASTER APPRENTICE MODEL

| | Master | Apprentice |
|---|---|---|
| Step 1 | Do | Watch |
| Step 2 | Do | Help |
| Step 3 | Help | Do |
| Step 4 | Watch | Do |

As you can see, this simple approach is both a mindset and a strategy. It's much better than jumping to step 3 or 4 and skipping over steps 1 and 2. When you skip over those steps, you're abdicating, not delegating, and you'll shortly find yourself taking over after the student fails to handle the process proficiently.

## WHEN DO YOU TRAIN PEOPLE ON THE SYSTEMS?

Recently, I was working with an operations manager of a growing construction company. Because his yard manager had recently quit, he found himself doing that person's job. I've seen too many situations where this happens. One person does another person's job for longer than desired and starts feeling burned out, frustrated, and resentful of having to work long hours. When you find yourself doing work that is not worth your hourly rate, it's time to delegate, outsource, or hire.

Commit to working on only your vital few activities that are critical to long-term success, satisfaction, and growth.

Your job as a leader is to develop the organizational structure, put the right people in the right seats, support them in developing systems that allow them to do their jobs, and enable them to elevate themselves in the organization. By creating a well-documented system to teach a replacement how to do their job, you are building a scalable company.

I don't mind if you have consultants, staff, or department leaders develop your systems. If someone else can do this activity well, then delegate it and focus on higher-value ones.

## THE FINISHED PRODUCT

Systems can take many forms. One of my first consulting jobs was to develop an operating manual for a contract flooring and carpet installation company that was installing about $30M worth of carpeting in new home developments in California annually. While developing their manual by interviewing employees and meticulously documenting their order fulfillment process, I came across the operating manual for Carl's Jr. It was three or four inches thick. I tried to achieve that same outcome for my client, but today, I would recommend otherwise. Today, an operating manual might include video recordings and computer screenshots showing how any and all processes (e.g., selling, delivering, and hiring) are to be documented, and it might live in cloud-based software for easy access.

## ACTION STEPS

1. Identify five to nine key processes that flow across departments/divisions/people and could use improvement because there are inconsistencies in how things are done.
2. Document those processes in enough detail for someone to follow them.
3. Begin to put an "Operations System Manual: How We Do Things around Here" type of workbook. It could be cloud-based, in video form, and stored on your shared drive.

CHAPTER 13

# PERFORMANCE

## MEASURING YOUR PROGRESS

*"So, this is the goal: To make money by increasing net profit, while simultaneously increasing return on investment, and simultaneously increasing cash flow."*

—ELIYAHU M. GOLDRATT, AUTHOR OF *THE GOAL: A PROCESS OF ONGOING IMPROVEMENT*, A BEST-SELLING BUSINESS NOVEL

I'm amazed by how many people don't understand their business financial statements. They don't understand the balance sheet. They are unfamiliar with the difference between cash flow and profit.

Most next-generation leaders going through a transition in the family ownership are probably taking over the books from their parents who made financial decisions "by the seat of their pants." But the disruptive successor knows that better optics on the financials leads to better decisions. And that better decisions lead to more money.

Most small business owners don't pay enough attention to financial ratios beyond the fundamental **profitability ratios** such as gross margin and net margin, which they often confuse. The other ratios include **liquidity ratios** (e.g., current ratio), **activity ratios** (e.g., accounts receivable turnover and inventory turnover), and **debt ratios** (e.g., debt to net worth). Typically, owners don't track these until a banking relationship with a line of credit or term loan is in place, and the bank requires them to pay attention to those measures so they don't violate any loan covenants.

Here are two more crucial measures of performance most family-business owners neglect. They are **return on equity** (net income ÷ owner's capital) and **return on investment** (net income ÷ total assets).

And finally, any business going through a transition will need to establish an **enterprise value** or **fair market value** to facilitate transfer of all or some of the company to the next generation of family members and shareholders.

Let's start with the basics first.

## THE BASIC THREE FINANCIAL STATEMENTS

I'm going to take you through the basics of financial management for family businesses, starting with three basic reports and the important things to know about them.

### THE INCOME STATEMENT

Let's begin with the income statement. The first thing most business owners get confused about is the difference between sales and revenue. Sales are orders taken and booked but not recognized. I prefer to think in terms of your sales pipeline and break that down into several categories: sales closed (dollar amounts), proposals out to clients, and prospects. We discussed this in the chapter on marketing and sales.

Next, be cognizant of your reporting basis. Is it cash or accrual? The main difference lies in the timing of when revenue and expenses are recognized. Cash is a more immediate recognition, whereas the accrual method focuses on anticipated income and expenses. The latter is more useful to managers. The former is used for paying your taxes.

The most critical items on the income statement are the top line, middle line, and bottom line because these break up the statement into readable chunks.

The top line is the revenue, but many statements show net revenue, too. An advertising agency may take a lot of fee income but then buy from media companies and keep only 15% of the fee income as commission. Such an agency has a lot of "pass-through" income and expenses. A client of mine provided independent investment advisors with asset management solutions, compliance oversight, and a technology platform. They were arguably a small business with under forty employees and top-line revenues of $40M. But 75% of that was pass-through income (commissions paid to registered investment advisors using their platform).

Because of the differences in revenue, net revenue and the cost of goods sold, the gross profit, which I call the middle line, matters more. The gross profit is what's left after you pay your direct costs for materials and typically your management labor, subcontract labor, and overhead expenses.

But here is where it gets tricky. Say you are a general contractor building homes, and your gross revenues are $3M/year. Let's say you have no employees and no materials costs because you use all subcontractors. If your subcontracted labor costs are $2.5M, then the gross profit is $500,000. That is what's left over for your management, overhead, and profit. As you can see, this $3M business suddenly looks like a much smaller company.

The bottom line—the net profit, operating profit, or EBITDA (earnings before interest, taxes, depreciation, and amortization)—can be misleading. Is this before or after the owner's compensation? Are many owner benefits (perks) buried in the financial statement?

It can be misleading to compare your business to another. Suppose you run the $3M general contractor business above, and you are making a 10% net profit of $300,000 after all your expenses. Since you run about $30,000/year of personal expenses through the business as owner benefit, and you earn a salary of $60,000, then $390,000 is the real owner's profit or discretionary earnings. To compare your performance against that of another firm, you need to know all of these details for them as well.

A healthy profit target for a business in a mature industry—and that would typically be any family business in the next generation—would be between 10% and 20%. Below a 10% net profit, you might be dangerously close to breakeven. If there's a contraction in the economy, like there has been every decade since the Great Depression of 1929, you could end up losing money. And if you're above 20 percent, new competitors will likely enter the industry due to its attractive profitability.

## THE BALANCE SHEET

It's called the balance sheet because it's an equation, which can be expressed several ways but is always shown in the following format:

> Assets = Liabilities + Owner's Equity (Net Worth)
>
> Assets (What You Have) - Liabilities (What You Owe) = What You Own (Owner's Equity)

This equation is always a snapshot of a point in time. Most commonly, we use it at the end of a month, quarter, or year. What is unique about the balance sheet is that it is a cumulative set of figures going back to the inception of the business. In contrast, the income statement represents only a specific period. The balance sheet helps you determine what you can borrow from outside sources (banks, commercial lenders) and whether you will need more capital from an equity source (angels, professional investors, private equity funds). It also shows how much you make on invested assets.

## THE CASH FLOW STATEMENT

The third financial statement, usually called the statement of cash flows, is largely underutilized. It is especially useful to companies that are growing fast, must manage their cash tightly, do not have an endless supply of capital, and find their assets getting tied up in materials, inventory, receivables, and deposits. Fast-growing businesses can outgrow their cash, and companies that are not well managed yet have significant assets can find themselves with healthy profits but no money to pay bills or buy more inventory or equipment. These problems require an understanding of cash flow and the elements that affect it.

There are three kinds of cash: cash from operating activities, cash from financing activities, and cash from investing activities. In other words, cash flow projections and statements virtually modify the net income to adjust for changes in working capital such as cash, accounts receivable and accounts payable, as well as changes in investments and borrowings before arriving at the net cash flow. For operators paying close attention to their cash flow, it is advisable to have financial management software and personnel, an accounting firm, or an outside advisor provide you with the three types of statements.

## HAVING GOOD FIGURES PAYS

Good financial statements offer a wealth of useful information. You don't need to be involved in producing the financial statements, but you need to understand how they are produced and what the numbers mean. First, if you're not confident in how your books are being done, change the people who are preparing them and have them document their processes so that a third party can make sure they make sense. After all, good numbers are critical to knowing how you are doing, which leads me to the first problem I encounter when working with many small, family-owned businesses.

I have seen too many financial statements that are prepared by a family member and are neither accurate nor useful to analyze for improvements, which is very frustrating to all, especially the business owner. Until this is fixed, it's difficult to advise or make decisions based on financial information.

Also, I've seen accountants and bookkeepers prepare financial period-ending statements yet provide no guidance on how to interpret them.

Finally, without providing all three financial statements to review, owners are looking at only part of the picture. Typically, they're looking only at the P&L statement, when they also need to be looking at the balance sheet and the cash flow.

Questions that arise from poor financial recordkeeping:

1. How are we doing compared to others in this industry?
2. How are we doing compared to last year?
3. What accounts are we making money on, and how much?
4. What accounts are we losing money on, and how much?

5. What is our profit margin on the different types of products/services we sell?
6. How do we implement job costing to know our profit per customer and profit per job?
7. What processes need to be improved?
8. How effectively are we utilizing our assets?
9. What is happening to our cash as we grow?
10. What is the relationship between our operating profit and operating cash flow?

## THE SECRET IS TO MONITOR YOUR RATIOS

To manage a business successfully, you need to pay attention to your growth rates and ratios. All business owners must pay attention to and carefully manage their profitability, leverage, and leverage and activity ratios. You also need to pay attention to your growth rates and their relationships to the three types of financial statements. Let's review them below.

### PROFITABILITY RATIOS

What are the gross profit, gross profit margin, net profit, and net profit margin of your business? If you have more than one division/department, break down the gross profit by division. The gross margin is the ratio of gross profit to gross revenues expressed as a percentage. Some business owners, when computing their pricing using a markup method, confuse margin and markup. It's critical to know they are inversely related. So if you mark up a product by 50% (from $100 to $150), your margin is 33% [($150 – 100)/$150].

When talking to friends or colleagues in your industry, you must know that they may be ignorant of how to speak about profitability and margins. The numbers don't lie unless they're inaccurate or fudged, but you have to see them to validate them.

When I promise prospective clients to help them achieve 3x average industry profitability, I know that the averages for most companies are pretty low. In 1991, the average profit margin across all industries was about 2 percent, according to my 1991 Risk Management Association (formerly Robert Morris Associates) Annual Statement Studies assembled for bankers. In a 2019 study by New York University Stern School of Business on public companies, it was 8% on the total market or 8.89% with financial statements. Because public companies, on average, have 4x the revenues and profitability per employee, I think it's reasonable to assume the profit margin of an average company to be about 3%. Achieving 3x industry average profitability may seem like a bold promise, but in reality, most private companies perform poorly.

That said, family businesses seem to perform much better than all other privately held companies. Although I don't have the data to support this, I believe the reasons are severalfold. One, more people are watching the books and "minding the business," so to speak. Two, people in family businesses tend to work harder because they care more about the company and the bottom line.

## LEVERAGE RATIOS

There are some critical figures to watch that are of great concern to business owners and bankers. The most important one is probably the debt-to-net worth ratio.

Total (Current and Long-Term) Debt ÷ Total Net Worth (Equity)

The **debt-to-net worth ratio** is a balance sheet measure where you take the total liabilities (in dollars) and divide that by the net worth (in dollars). The higher the **ratio**, the higher the percentage of your total capital is financed by **debt**. A healthy business uses leverage intelligently. A small business with a ratio of debt to equity greater than 5:1 would be considered highly leveraged. It would probably require some sort of government guarantee, such as provided by the SBA (Small Business Administration) to secure a bank loan.

Another important leverage ratio to pay attention to is the times service coverage ratio, which measures the ratio of net profit to interest expense. Lenders like to see a ratio greater than 1.5:1—that is, $1.50 of profit for every $1.00 of interest expense.

## LIQUIDITY RATIOS

Other ratios measure the solvency or liquidity of your business, which indicates whether you are a "going concern." The current ratio is the most important one, as it measures how many dollars of current assets you have to pay off current liabilities. It is expressed as follows:

Current Ratio = Current Assets ÷ Current Liabilities

Net working capital is defined as current assets minus current liabilities.

### ACTIVITY RATIOS

Activity ratios measure how quickly you turn over assets such as receivables, payables, and inventory. Days sales outstanding measures how many days on average it takes to collect from your customers. Days payable outstanding shows how many days on average it takes to pay your customers. Inventory turnover ratios show how many times you turn your inventory each year.

Averages are essential to know and compare against because your customers will see them as the norm. They will base their decisions to do business or continue to do business with you on how your business compares to the competition. When you perform above the norm, you can generate cash better, which gives you more flexibility in your management.

Let's look at inventory turnover for a moment. Suppose your typical retail clothing store turns its inventory four times per year, which means they will usually have ninety days of stock on hand. If they can turn it twelve times per year, they will need only thirty days of inventory on hand. The business that turns its stock faster will be much more efficient in its use of capital because it doesn't need to have cash tied up in inventory. Suppose you have a business such as a nursery for growing trees. Your stock might mature over time and be with you several years before you sell it. The key factor in this situation is that the tree gets more valuable the longer you hold it.

## THE ULTIMATE BLUEPRINT FOR AN INSANELY SUCCESSFUL BUSINESS

I told you earlier I would discuss the importance of growth rates and their relationship with the three financial statements.

Keith J. Cunningham, the author of *The Ultimate Blueprint for an Insanely Successful Business* and creator of the CFO Scoreboard software, sums it up perfectly. He says the secret is simply that "you need to be very effective at acquiring assets that maximize and service revenue, then be very efficient at converting those revenues into profits, and finally be very productive at converting profits into cash flow."

Keith continues to explain: "When it comes to the blueprint for your business, you have to pay close attention to not only the size of each number but also the growth rates. You don't want—on a percentage basis—assets to grow faster than your revenues. If this happens, your assets are becoming less and less effective. You don't want your revenues—on a percentage basis—to grow faster than your profits. When this happens, your revenues are becoming less and less efficient. And you don't want your profits—on a percentage basis—to grow faster than your operating cash flow. If this is the case, your profits are becoming less and less productive. There could be short periods where one of the above scenarios occurs, but in the long term, any of the above trends are deadly.

"In a well-run business, you want to cascade your percentage growth rates so that operating cash flow is growing faster than profits, profits are growing faster than revenues, and revenues are growing faster than assets (regardless of whether those assets are buildings, machinery, people, or payroll dollars)."[19]

## TYING IT ALL TOGETHER WITH THE STRATEGIC PROFIT FORMULA

The strategic profit formula (another name for the DuPont equation) provides a method to understand your return on net worth. To calculate your return on net worth, you need to look at these two distinct measures: return on assets (ROA) and return on equity (ROE). ROA looks at how efficiently management is using its total assets to generate profits. ROE measures how much profit your company makes from each dollar of owner's equity.

These two return on investment ratios are driven by three performance ratios: profit margin, asset turnover, and financial leverage. Each of them represents a pathway or strategy to improve return on investment and is valuable in analyzing performance.

Below are the strategic profit formula figures for a typical construction business. The second half of the equation covers your financial leverage, which shows the extent to which debt (leverage) is used in the company's capital structure.

| | | | |
|---|---|---|---|
| **Path 1** | Profit Margin | **5.5%** | $\frac{\text{Profit Before Taxes}}{\text{Net Sales}}$ |
| **Path 2** | Asset Turnover | × **3.5** | $\frac{\text{Net Sales}}{\text{Totat Assets}}$ |
| | Return on Assets | = **19.25%** | $\frac{\text{Profit Before Taxes}}{\text{Total Assets}}$ |
| **Path 3** | Financial Leverage | × **1.75** | $\frac{\text{Total Assets}}{\text{Net Worth}}$ |
| | Return on Net Worth | = **33.68%** | $\frac{\text{Profit Before Taxes}}{\text{Net Worth}}$ |

## 33.68% RETURN ON NET WORTH

Now that you can see what the ROE (return on net worth) is from your investment in your business, you can evaluate whether to invest an additional $100,000 into your business or to invest it elsewhere. As you can see, the ROE is ultimately most important. In the equation, you can see that this business provides a 19.25% return on investment and a 33.68% ROE. In other words, for every $100,000 invested in the company, you will get $133,680—an excellent return on your investment. Given a choice between investing in your privately held business or the publicly held markets, would you choose your company? Unless you are already heavily invested in your business and wish to diversify your holdings, I'm guessing the answer is "Absolutely!"

By understanding this formula, you can model changes to profit margin, asset turnover, and financial leverage to see which levers have the most significant impact on your returns on your investment and your equity.

## KEY PERFORMANCE INDICATORS (KPIS)

To achieve your desired outcomes or lagging indicators—e.g., net profit or ROA—you should manage and measure your activities or leading indicators. By controlling the right things as you go, you'll get to your desired results—as in the case above, a 33.68% return on invested capital.

Typically, most companies will look at some similar measures, which ultimately will translate to the desired outcomes. (Most companies focus on Path 1, Profit Margin. A few focus on Path 2, Asset Turnover and Path 3, Financial Leverage.) But selecting the right indicators and choosing a mix of leading and lagging indicators will help you achieve the desired result. When working with clients, I frequently pull out my list of 561 KPIs, which has the most commonly selected KPIs bolded. Since this topic alone could be the subject of an entire book, I am going to keep this simple.

Typically, business owners measure revenue per employee but not the more critical gross profit per employee or the even more useful profit per employee. Often, in mature industries, it's easy to find the averages of these figures in industry magazines or studies, so you can start by benchmarking your business against your industry or region. I have helped many contractors in the landscape industry make massive improvements in their results just by trying to beat industry averages.

Many companies I work with have revenues between $100,000 and $200,000 per employee and profits of 10–20% that figure. By contrast, large, well-branded companies, which have pricing power, can have revenues per employee of $400,000+. And the best companies such as Apple crush those figures; Apple had a profit per employee of $451,000 in 2018, which is just under the average revenue per employee for the top companies worldwide!

It's hard to say whether it's best to start by benchmarking your company against competitors or against yourself. It's like golf in that your focus is best placed on your game and not someone else's. But the primary measures of how your company is performing compared to others in your industry (and in other industries) are undoubtedly essential and helpful to know because they show you what is possible.

## THE POWER OF BUDGETING

Most experts agree, to accomplish your financial goals, let's say a 15–20% net profit at year-end, you'll need to create a budget and adjust it periodically by creating some pro forma financial statements. Setting an intention to strive toward forces you to manage your finances better. The exercise of preparing a budget sets you and the team up to prepare for a specific result. Once you have identified that result, you can then monitor your actual progress versus your budget and make course corrections along the way.

The reason this is important is that it helps you hit your target. Say that you want to get from Los Angeles to New York driving in a car. Would you depart without setting a course first? Certainly not. You set your path, and you course correct as conditions present themselves. Say you suddenly find yourself driving toward traffic. With proper guidance and advance information, you can course correct to avoid these obstacles. The same goes for your financial statements—you can course correct by examining your monthly performance. Look at the variance items and percentages. This way, you can prepare for course corrections in the coming month.

Each quarter, my clients and I meet, away from the workplace, to get perspective and set intentions for the upcoming quarter. We do this only after we have looked in the rearview mirror to see where we came from and how well we did. My clients use a quarterly planner tool to help them stay focused on their ninety-day, twelve-month, and three- to five-year goals. We review how well we performed against these and look ahead to factors that may impact our future results or cause us to change direction.

By maintaining a rolling twelve-month trailing budget with a revised forecast, you can stay on top of everything. Using Microsoft Excel, Google Sheets, or even a simple accounting program, you can create your budgets and revised forecasts.

### ACTION STEPS

1. You need to understand your financial statements: know how to read an income statement, balance sheet, and cash flow.
2. If you don't have talented financial help, you need to hire someone you can trust and to answer your questions.
3. Calculate your return on investment and return on equity in your business using the strategic profit model.
4. Develop monthly or quarterly budgets for your income and expenses, balance sheet, and cash flow.

## CHAPTER 14

# BEGIN WITH THE END IN MIND

*"To begin with the end in mind means to start with a clear understanding of your destination. It means to know where you're going so that you better understand where you are now and so that the steps you take are always in the right direction."*

—STEPHEN R. COVEY, AUTHOR OF *THE 7 HABITS OF HIGHLY EFFECTIVE PEOPLE* AND FOUNDER OF FRANKLIN-COVEY

Before Justin of K&D came to me, he didn't have a roadmap for growth or a mentor to guide him through defining his vision. He knew he wanted to build a business by design, not by default. He knew his vision was what mattered. But he didn't yet see that beginning with the end in mind would define the plan. In one of our coaching sessions, we mapped out the financial path to getting to $30M, which neatly had us getting there by 2030, giving us a BHAG® mantra of "$30M by 2030."

Mapping out a plan is what explorers do when they are preparing for their journeys, which is why I love the stories of Roald Amundsen's, Robert Falcon Scott's, and Sir Ernest Shackleton's trips to the South Pole. These were journeys of epic proportions in which explorers competed to be the first humans to reach the South Pole in the early 1900s, which we now know as the heroic age of Antarctic exploration.

Habit #2 from *The 7 Habits of Highly Effective People* teaches that the work ahead of you, not behind you, is always your most important work. The mental creation of your business comes first, followed by the physical creation, just as a building follows a blueprint. And this is what business coaches do for our clients. We take a stand for the client's future state and help them get where they're going faster and with more ease.

Do you have a vision for your business five, ten, twenty, or more years from now? Do you think you will want to sell it or pass it on to another generation of family members?

This chapter is about how to build to sell and exit gracefully so that your business doesn't end up like the 70% of family-owned businesses that fail to make the intergenerational transfer OR the 70–80% that fail to sell[20] OR the 75% of businesses whose owners regret selling one year later.[21]

## IS THERE AN EXIT PLAN IN YOUR MIND?

The fact is that 100% of business owners will leave their businesses. Eventually. One way or the other. But did you know almost a third (30.5 percent) of family business owners have no plans to ever retire and nearly another third (29.2 percent) report that retirement is more than eleven years away?[22] The fact that so many owners plan to live out all their years in the office poses unique challenges to the succeeding generation. Then there's the 79% of business owners who plan to exit their businesses in the next ten years—and the 75% who would exit today if their financial security were assured.[23] These are some stark statistics and may explain why you, as a disruptive successor, feel like you are wrestling the business away from the founder.

You can give yourself options by developing a clear exit plan when you begin, communicating your intention to family members, and working hard to drive value in the business so that it is buyer and seller ready when the time comes. When you're ready to retire, everything will be prepared for you to make the transition a successful one.

In 1985, at age nineteen, Chris Sugai founded Solar Art, a Los Angeles-based window film installation company. In 2005, while running Solar Art full time, he founded Niner Bikes, a mountain bike manufacturing company that he was excited to grow. When Chris was a member of my CEO peer group, we identified that he had no clear successor for his window film company. His general manager didn't have the resources to buy the business. I helped Chris improve the value and "sell-ability" of his window film company. I introduced him to a successful business broker who guided him through the sale of that company so he could focus his efforts on the mountain bike business. A few years later, Niner Bikes made it onto the *Inc.* magazine 5,000 fastest-growing companies list. So selling the window film business was the right choice and gave him the confidence and cash to focus all his efforts on Niner Bikes. He exited, devoted himself to the bike businesses, moved out of California, and never looked back.

## BUILD YOUR BOAT (BUSINESS OWNERS ADVISORY TEAM)

Your BOAT may also be your exit planning advisory team. Typically, this team comprises trusted, professional advisors such as your accountant, attorney, wealth manager, insurance agent, exit planning advisor, and business coach. Each of these people plays an essential and distinct role in the planning, value creation, and transfer process.

Before your parent(s) transfer(s) the ownership of the business to you, you will both want to make sure you have a team in place to support and advise you through the transition and beyond. You'll need advisors knowledgeable about business and succession planning, both to protect the value of the business and to distribute it to the new shareholders. You'll probably want to hire an accountant, a financial advisor, or a valuation company to determine the value of the company and the methodology you'll use to update it going forward. A financial planner would be helpful to advise your parent(s) on their financial requirements and plans, since the business was likely their principal asset. And a financial advisor or wealth manager can help you invest and continue to compound the growth of any investable assets. An insurance advisor can help structure some tax-deferred executive compensation plans for the next generation. I also recommend you hire someone like myself, a family-friendly business coach, to mediate all parties' interests while helping to drive enterprise value before, during, and after the transition. You might consider adding to your BOAT one to two industry friends, mentors, or peers who have been through this process before. This small group of five to seven people whom you might meet with quarterly/semiannually/annually or contact one-on-one as needed, can be constructive in driving value in the business as you continue to grow.

## THE PLAN-DO-CHECK-ACT CYCLE

A written transition plan may be helpful. With the help of an exit planner, you can develop a written plan that outlines the exit strategy, governance and family systems, growth planning, execution and accountability, succession planning, and leadership skills development.

The business transition planning model shown below follows a plan-do-check-act (PDCA) approach:

**BUSINESS TRANSITION PLANNING MODEL**

**EXIT** STRATEGY

**GOVERNANCE** AND FAMILY SYSTEMS

**GROWTH** PLANNING

**EXECUTION** AND ACCOUNTABILITY

**SUCCESSION** PLANNING

**LEADERSHIP** SKILLS DEVELOPMENT

## THE EIGHT DRIVERS OF VALUE IN GROWTH PLANNING

Driving growth over the life of the business and through the exit planning process should always be a top priority. Transition planning should never distract you from your main objective in the business, which is driving value.

John Warrillow, founder of The Value Builder System™ and author of *Built to Sell* and *The Automatic Customer*, breaks down eight drivers of company value that impact transferability and the owners' ability to sell for a premium. An understanding of these drivers will help you and your BOAT, especially your business coach, focus on what matters most in value creation, whether it's increasing the multiple on earnings, growing the company, creating a recurring revenue stream, or one of the other drivers. Here's a summary of the eight value drivers that make up the foundation of The Value Builder System™:

1. **Financial performance**, specifically the size of your revenues along with your past and expected future profitability, is the number one driver of value in most businesses, especially those with under $20M in revenues. A financial acquirer sees buying a business as paying today for a stream of profits in the future, which is why companies are generally bought and sold based on a multiple of their earnings. When valuing a business, financial buyers will typically value not only the next year's profit but also all profits expected in the foreseeable future. For every year into the future they must wait for their expected return on their investment, they will "discount" the future profit the current owners are projecting.
2. **Growth potential** is another driver of value; what is the potential for the business to grow at the time of valuation? If it's likely possible to increase your number of customers, your sales to existing customers, your average sale size, or your frequency of purchase, this will add to the value of your business.
3. **Monopoly control:** Warren Buffett is famous for investing in companies with a protective "moat" around them. The wider and deeper the moat, the harder it is for competitors to compete. An enduring competitive advantage also gives an owner more control over pricing, which increases both

profitability and cash flow. By staking a claim to something that is unique and meaningful to customers, you can differentiate your business from competitors.

4. Supplier, employee, and customer independence: To be salabe, a business must not be overly reliant on any one customer, employee, or supplier. If your business is too dependent on one or two key suppliers, companies, or consultants, you are at their mercy. Likewise, if you are too reliant on any one employee, you are at significant risk if they choose to leave or negotiate their salary. If your business is dependent on any one customer, it can become highly unstable at any time.
5. **Recurring revenue:** One of the most significant factors in determining the value of your company is the extent to which an acquirer can see where your sales will come from in the future. If your business requires that you start from scratch each month, the value of your company will be lower than if you can predict the sources and amount of your future revenues. A recurring revenue stream, like that of a commercial landscape maintenance business, subscription service, or business with managed services contracts, lets you see months, even years into the future. Therefore, creating an annuity stream is the best way to increase the value of your business.
6. **Customer satisfaction:** Acquirers care about the extent to which your customers are satisfied and your ability to assess their satisfaction consistently and rigorously. Most business owners know intuitively how satisfied their customers are, but as their companies grow, some lose touch with their customers. Being able to measure the satisfaction of your customers is essential to maintaining their loyalty, which correlates with future predictability of revenues and cash flow.

7. **Cash flow positive:** Many companies, as they grow, suck up cash rather than generate net cash flow. For example, a company that sells a product requiring inventory of parts can need more capital as they grow. The same is true of companies whose money gets tied up in accounts receivable. The more cash an acquirer must inject into your company when taking it over, the less they will pay for it. The inverse is also true: the less cash your acquirer must deposit into your business, the higher the price they will pay.
8. **Owner dependency:** If your business is highly dependent on you, the value of your company to an acquirer goes down. Your business must be able to grow without you. The more your customers need you and ask for you, the harder it is to grow your business, and the less valuable your company will be in the long run. Therefore, it is wise to build a company with a second-in-command. This person may not have your vision, but there are countless examples of second-in-command leaders who have taken their companies to new heights. Google, Apple, and Microsoft have grown tremendously under their second-in-commands' leadership.

## BUSINESS VALUE EXPLAINED

So what's your business worth? Valuing a business is typically done by using a combination of methods and taking the weighted average of the answers they produce. These methods include:

1. Discounted cash flow
2. Rule-of-thumb multiples of earnings, cash flow, or discretionary seller earnings

3. Asset replacement value
4. Market comparable

Ultimately, a business is only worth what someone will pay for it, and commonly, the terms and conditions of a transfer or sale are as crucial as the value.

Typically, for smaller companies considering a transition from one generation to another, hiring a CPA is enough to get a fair value. At the same time, an appraisal or valuation firm is recommended by experts when a more precise figure for estate and tax purposes is needed.

If you're planning to transition the business to family members, you'll want to hire an independent firm to value the company and another to advise you through the transition. You should anticipate issues such as compensation for officers, principal shareholders, and family members, along with stock ownership, dividend distribution policies, and more.

Before your contribution to the business declines in value, it's best to plan well so that fair value can be had by all.

## THE FOUNDER'S EXIT OPTIONS

A founder usually has more than one exit option. The choices might include:

- Sell or exit via sale to an individual financial buyer
- Sell or exit via merger/acquisition with a strategic buyer
- Sell or exit via an initial public offering (IPO)
- Sell to your employees using an employee stock option plan (ESOP)

- Transfer to family members via a purchase over time (installment sale)
- Transfer to family members via a leveraged buyout using outside capital
- Transfer to family members using the lifetime gifting exemptions
- Hire a family member or trusted person to run the business and stay on as a consultant
- Shut down/liquidate

Before they consider their exit, they will want to get clear on their reasons for exiting the business. Are they being pulled to do something else, such as spending time with family, traveling, starting another business, or empowering the next generation? Or are they feeling pushed out due to age, burnout, or changing market conditions? Consider whether you are being pulled or pushed, as either choice can have a remarkable impact on the selling price, process, and experience.

In a family business, there are often different stakeholder groups to consider. Remember John Davis's Family Business System model? Carefully finding each constituency's expectations and needs will be necessary during the transfer process.

## THE EXIT PLANNING PROCESS

The exit planning process allows owners to see their business from the perspective of their disruptive successor or a potential buyer. As with any planning process, the goal is to maximize enterprise value by working with value sources—the tangible and intangible assets.

Given the exit planning process can take three to five years or more, owners should start the process early so that financial security is assured. In family businesses, succession planning is emphasized in the exit planning process. Succession planning is a subcomponent of exit planning and refers to the selection (including possibly a new hire), training, and retention of a successor CEO.

When a business is sold, a business broker, M&A advisor, or intermediary will be the quarterback and will marshal resources as needed, such as a lawyer, accountant, real estate broker, or valuation advisor. When a family business is transferred to the next generation, a trusted business advisor, business coach, or exit planner will instead marshal these resources.

Something to know during the transition plan is that your parent can use their lifetime gifting exemption to transfer the business. Consult with your CPA about current exemption limits and requirements. Also, in most cases, the founders will want to do this gradually as you take increasing responsibility for business results. There is no right age to transfer a company. The age and desires of your parent(s) may dictate the circumstances. The truth is that when you are adding more value to the company than your parent is, it is time to transfer control.

## ACTION STEPS

1. Obtain a business valuation from a professional if you want to determine the value for gifting purposes or to prepare for an inside sale/transfer.
2. Calculate how much money you need from the sale or transfer.

3. Create an exit plan and think through the succession steps in the model.
4. Identify people and positions to take over vital functions and business responsibilities as you scale up.

# CHAPTER 15

# THE FUTURE IS NOW

*"It's what you learn after you know it all that counts."*

—JOHN WOODEN, UCLA BASKETBALL COACH, NICKNAMED THE WIZARD OF WESTWOOD FOR HIS LESSONS ON LEADERSHIP AND WINNING

Family businesses, in many senses, are like other businesses. However, they are often more loyal to their employees because they are a family first, and they are unique in that they have many different stakeholder groups to satisfy. Rivalries must be resolved for the business to sustain itself.

I frequently meet next-generation leaders who are running the family business but still have a parent participating in the ongoing management of the company. They want to make decisions, such as replacing longtime employees, but they are uncomfortable doing so. Waiting for a parent's permission is holding them back—probably holding the business back from growth and profitability, too.

If your parent is involved in managing the business and you would like your voice to be heard, NOW is the time to share your vision and lead.

Remember what I said earlier?

Between 60 and 70% of family business leaders would like to pass their business on to the next generation, and more importantly, 39% will pass it on within the next five years. But only 30% will be successful at transitioning to the next generation, which is why you need to step in now and disrupt the business leadership but not the family relationships.

Taking leadership in a time of intergenerational transfer can be a painful rite of passage. Given the rate of failure of family businesses, doing everything you can to prepare yourself for this transfer is critical. Having a playbook or methodology provides the support necessary to ensure your 7 P's (purpose, planning, products, people, priorities, processes, and performance) are well crafted and understood by all. It sets the stage for a successful transition from one generation to another.

The disruptive successor must admit that their primary teacher—their parent—can no longer get the business where it needs to go. The disruptive successor must leverage additional external resources to grow, including business books, peer learning opportunities, advisors, mentors, and coaches. During the transition from one generation to the next, successors who commit to learning and applying their knowledge to the business find the most success. After all, the best learning happens when you use what you've learned.

My 7 P's Playbook is your checklist to run your business.

When Justin White became a client, he was seeking help to prepare himself for taking over the family business. He knew that to get where he wanted it to go, the company would need new processes and people who could grow the business with him. His parents did a great job raising him to be a person of character, competence, and intelligence. Still, they didn't have the business acumen that he needed to learn to build his company into an eight-figure business. He knew that what got the company where it was would not get it where he wanted it to be. He sought outside help—just as this book is outside help for you—to set him on his path to 10x growth. With all systems optimized, it was only a handful of years before he achieved that goal.

You can do it, too! Justin is just one example of many next-generation leaders who are disruptive successors. You just have to want to make a massive difference in the world around you—your family, your employees, your customers, your community, and your shareholders.

So we've come to an end. You have my 7 P's Playbook and can start working systematically through each chapter using the tools and concepts I've discussed. Your application of the framework is where the real learning begins.

So go to www.DisruptiveSuccessor.com, download the current tools, and complete the action steps at the end of each chapter. Start today to position your family's business to make a successful transition between generations and begin to grow for the future.

Then take the most crucial step of all. Share the strategies in this book with your team and family members by sharing the book itself with them. Do this so you are all on the same page. Do this so you are all committed to implementing the changes that will make your company reach the heights of success you all want it to.

## ACTION STEPS

The first things you need to do to achieve the success you want are:

1. Develop your mindset to act strategically. Focus your energy and your power by developing mental, physical, and emotional health. This is fundamental to getting the right things done faster. Create routines and habits that amplify your focus by setting up your calendar with productive work blocks at high productivity times such as first thing in the morning.
2. Take an inventory of your people, their talents, and their fit for the functions you need filled. Do you have the right people on your team? That is, do they share your core values? Are they in the correct seats in your company's organizational structure? Are they doing the right things? Are they clear on their roles and how they are being evaluated?
3. Do you have a written one-page plan that is visible to others on the team to foster alignment with them? Does everyone have clarity about the company's number one priority and their individual and departmental priorities for the upcoming quarter and year? If not, schedule a retreat to work on developing this plan, affirming the priorities and people on the team and elevating your habits to focus on your vital few activities. Schedule your meeting rhythm—daily, weekly, monthly, quarterly, annual, and family board meetings—to ensure follow-up and follow-through.
4. Go back through each chapter and find the tools you need to work on each P in the Leader's Playbook.
5. Contact me if you need further help. I offer a free sequence of calls to understand your challenges/issues and explore what working together would look like.

# ACKNOWLEDGMENTS

Writing a book is never an easy task. Although it didn't take me long to write it, relatively speaking, it took years of learning and coaching to get me to the place where I was ready to write it. In other words, many people have contributed along the way.

I want to thank those coaches who have nudged me: Paul Lemberg, who gave me the methodology to write a book fast, and Michael Cody, who inspired me to write on this subject in the first place, gave me editorial critique, improved on the structure, and helped me as I approached the finish line.

There are many coaching organizations and individuals to whom I am indebted because they introduced me to the power of coaching businesses and gave me tools and proven systems to work with entrepreneurs and family business leaders. These include Scaling Up, Gazelles International, EOS® Worldwide, The Coaches' Coach, and The Growth Coach.

I would also like to shout out people such as Patrick Lencioni of The Table Group, John Warrillow of Value Builder System, Simon Sinek of Simon Sinek Inc., and Peter F. Drucker for his pearls of wisdom, which have influenced so many of us. I have learned from many people along my journey to becoming an experienced coach of the multimillion-dollar, family-owned, and privately held entrepreneurial business. If I left you out, forgive me.

Thank you, Justin, for allowing me to share your story so freely; having you as a client has been rewarding on so many levels. And to my maternal grandfather, Wilfred "Willie" P. Cohen, a "self-made man" who, despite his size (5′ 1″), lived tall in the most magnificent city in the world—New York—and in the annals of men's suits, art, and philanthropy.

Finally, to my father, who joined the family business, Joseph H. Cohen & Sons, but passed at the age of thirty-five, when I was two years old. His passing left me with a constant drive to balance work with play. Had he known his fate, he might have quoted B. C. Forbes, founder of *Forbes* magazine, who said, "Don't forget until too late that the business of life is not business but living."

# ABOUT THE AUTHOR

**JONATHAN GOLDHILL** is a master coach, educator, and expert guide in personal and business growth who has been leading his clients—closely held and family-owned businesses—since 1987. His passion for advising entrepreneurs and family businesses ignited a year earlier when his family's business, one of the largest manufacturers of men's clothing in the United States, ceased operations and failed to survive into the fourth generation of family ownership.

Jonathan has owned or managed several businesses, which have grown into multimillion-dollar companies, including VEDC in Los Angeles, which grew from a fledgling organization into the largest business and economic development firm in the region. Some of his clients, including Anchor Loans, FPA Technology Services, King's Hawaiian bakery, K&D Landscaping, and Niner Bikes, have achieved double-digit growth in their sales and profitability and have been featured on lists of the fastest-growing companies and best places to work.

He is the author of *Weathering the Pandemic Storm*, *The 6 Silver Bullets to Growing Any Business's Profits Fast*, *Weathering the Economic Storm*, *Sales Accelerator: Strikingly Simple & Effective*

*Strategies for Today's Marketing*, and numerous articles on business growth, family business, and value creation. Jonathan has certificates in coaching and an MBA in entrepreneurship and management consulting from the University of Southern California.

More info about the author and his services can be found at www.TheGoldhillGroup.com.

To download and share a free chapter of the book, go to www.DisruptiveSuccessor.com.

# NOTES

Sometimes people are interested in knowing the sources of information to learn more but don't want to feel like there are so many that it's like reading a research paper. So I've limited it to under twenty-five external references.

1 BHAG is a registered trademark of Jim Collins, author of several books including *Built to Last*, *Good to Great*, *Great by Choice*, and others.

2 Conway Center for Family Business, "Family Business Facts," https://www.familybusinesscenter.com/resources/family-business-facts/.

3 PWC, "2019 US Family Business Survey," https://www.pwc.com/us/en/industries/private-company-services/library/family-business-survey.html.

4 "The Botany 500 Building: Failure of Garment Square," https://botany500building-philly-blog.tumblr.com/.

5 Dan Roth, "Where's the Business Selling 'Tsunami'?" International Business Group LLC (dba IBG Business), https://ibgbusiness.com/wheres-the-business-selling-tsunami/.

6 Mass Mutual, "Mass Mutual American Family Business Survey, 2007," http://www.massmutual.com/mmfg/pdf/afbs.pdf.

7 PWC, "2016 Family Business Survey," http://www.pwc.com/gx/en/services/family-business/family-business-survey-2016.html.

8 For a more detailed approach, read Ami Kassar, *The Growth Dilemma: Determining Your Entrepreneurial Type to Find Your Financing Comfort Zone* (New York: An Inc. Original, 2018).

9 Joy McGovern, Michael Lindemann, Monica Vergara, Stacey Murphy, Linda Barker, and Rodney Warrenfeltz, "Maximizing the Impact of Executive Coaching: Behavioral Change, Organizational Outcomes, and Return on Investment," *The Manchester Review: A Journal for People and Organizations in Transition* 6, no. 1 (2001).

10 This statement was given by Donald Rumsfeld on February 12, 2002, during a US Department of Defense news briefing about the lack of evidence linking the government of Iraq with the supply of weapons of mass destruction to terrorist groups.

11 Peter Drucker, *Management: Tasks, Responsibilities and Practices* (New York: Harper & Row, 1974), 6.

12 OECD, Organisation of Economic Co-operation and Development, is an intergovernmental economic organization with thirty-seven member countries founded in 1961 to stimulate economic progress and world trade.

13 Operating Cost Study for the Green Industry, prepared by Profit Planning Group for the National Association of Landscape Professionals.

14 Source: Professor Mike Smith, University of Manchester, UK, August 1994. John E. Hunter and Ronda R. Hunter, "Validity and Utility of Alternative Predictors of Job Performance," *Psychology Bulletin* 96 (1994).

15 Gallup Poll, "2015 Employee Engagement Source," https://news.gallup.com/poll/188144/employee-engagement-stagnant-2015.aspx.

16 Britt Andreatta, "Calculating the Cost of Employee Attrition and Disengagement," LinkedIn Learning Course, https://learning.linkedin.com/content/dam/me/learning/en-us/pdfs/lil-workbook-calculating-cost-of-employee-attrition-and-disengagement.pdf.

17 Source: TTI Success Insights®, Emotional Quotient™ © 2020 by Dr. Izzy Justice and Target Training International, Ltd.

18 Permission granted by the author. The Three-Circle Model of the Family Business System was developed by Renato Tagiuri and John Davis at Harvard Business School and was circulated in working papers starting in 1978. It was first published in Davis's doctoral dissertation, "The Influence of Life Stages on Father-Son Work Relationships in Family Companies," in 1982. In 1996, *Family Business Review* published it in Tagiuri and Davis's classic article, "Bivalent Attributes of the Family Firm."

19 Keith J. Cunningham, *The Ultimate Blueprint for an Insanely Successful Business* (City: Keys to the Vault, 2011), chap. 4.

20 T. West, *Business Reference Guide: The Essential Guide Pricing Businesses and Franchises* (Wilmington, NC: Business Brokerage Press, 2015).

21 Exit Planning Institute, "Owner's Readiness to Exit Survey," 2013.

22 Cornell SC Johnson College of Business, "Family Business Facts," https://www.johnson.cornell.edu/smith-family-business-initiative-at-cornell/resources/family-business-facts/.

23 Business Enterprise Institute (BEI), "2016 Business Owner Survey Report," https://www.exitplanning.com/2016-business-owner-survey-report.